PINOCHET

F

THEMATIC STUDIES IN LATIN AMERICA

Series editor: Gilbert W. Merkx,
Director, Latin American Institute,
University of New Mexico

THE POLITICAL ECONOMY OF
REVOLUTIONARY NICARAGUA
by Rose J. Spalding

WOMEN ON THE U.S.-MEXICO BORDER:
RESPONSES TO CHANGE
edited by Vicki L. Ruiz and Susan Tiano

THE JEWISH PRESENCE IN LATIN AMERICA
edited by Judith Laikin Elkin and Gilbert W. Merkx

POLICYMAKING IN MEXICO: FROM BOOM TO CRISIS
by Judith A. Teichman

LAND, POWER, AND POVERTY:
AGRARIAN TRANSFORMATION AND
POLITICAL CONFLICT IN CENTRAL AMERICA
by Charles D. Brockett

PINOCHET: THE POLITICS OF POWER
by Genaro Arriagada. *Translated by* Nancy Morris

THE WOMEN'S MOVEMENT IN LATIN AMERICA
FEMINISM AND THE TRANSITION TO DEMOCRACY
edited by Jane S. Jaquette

THE CHILEAN POLITICAL PROCESS
by Manuel Antonio Garreton

Additional titles under preparation.

PINOCHET

The Politics of Power

Genaro Arriagada

Translated by Nancy Morris
with
Vincent Ercolano and Kristen A. Whitney

Westview Press
BOULDER • SAN FRANCISCO • OXFORD

Copyright © 1991 by Westview Press, Inc.

Published in 1991 in the United States of America by Westview Press, Inc., 5500 Central Avenue, Boulder, Colorado 80301, and in the United Kingdom by Westview Press, 36 Lonsdale Road, Summertown, Oxford OX2 7EW

First published in 1988 by Unwin Hyman, Inc.

Library of Congress Cataloging-in-Publication Data available upon request

ISBN 0-8133-1266-3

Printed and bound in the United States of America

The paper used in this publication meets the requirements of the American National Standard for Permanence of Paper for Printed Library Materials Z39.48-1984.

10   9   8   7   6   5   4   3   2

CONTENTS

FOREWORD

The military regime of General Augusto Pinochet Ugarte is anomalous, whether viewed from a comparatively international perspective or considered in terms of Chilean history. From a comparative perspective, the Pinochet regime stands out as a remarkably durable and personalistic dictatorship in a politically sophisticated and relatively modernized country. From a Chilean viewpoint, Pinochet's regime represents an extraordinary break with the traditions that have characterized Chilean public life and state institutions for most of the country's history.

The Pinochet regime was established in 1973 by one of the bloodiest military takeovers to mark Latin American history in the two decades following the Cuban Revolution. By the time of the Chilean coup, most of Latin America had fallen under military rule, including such relatively modernized countries as Brazil and Uruguay. The new military regimes were defined not by loyalty to a particular dictator but by an institutional reaction against popular-sector pressures, revolutionary threats, and economic crisis. In the words of the distinguished Argentine social scientist Gullermo O'Donnell, these regimes were "bureaucratic-authoritarian" in nature, not the personalistic dictatorships considered characteristic of more backward countries.

By the mid-1980s the military governments of Latin America had largely disappeared. The bureaucratic-authoritarian regimes had become victims of economic and political disasters of their own making, while the more traditional dictatorships of Somoza in Nicaragua and the Duvalier dynasty in Haiti fell to the forces of change. Only two regimes survived intact from the 1970s: the long-standing dictatorship of General Alfredo Stroessner in Paraguay and the Pinochet regime in Chile, which was originally viewed by most observers as a clearcut example of the bureaucratic-authoritarian model.

The Pinochet regime has not avoided the policy blunders that brought down the once-contemporaneous military regimes in Argentina, Brazil, Uruguay, and elsewhere. No regime applied free-market economics with greater rigor and perseverance, and no country suffered a deeper financial crisis, more unemployment, or greater deindustrialization than Chile under Pinochet. Moreover, no regime has shown a greater disdain for international opinion concerning human rights violations. Nevertheless, Pinochet survived when his fellow dictators could not, despite the massive mobilization of opposition forces in Chile.

Pinochet's tenure seems even more noteworthy from a Chilean perspective. Before the coup of 1973, Pinochet himself was seen as a legalistic officer upholding a constitutionalist military tradition that was rare in Latin America and the subject of considerable national pride. The growing sense of crisis and polarization that marked the Popular Unity government of Salvador Allende had led to significant support for military intervention on the assumption that Chile would return to constitutional rule after a brief military interregnum. Few supporters of the intervention expected neither the violence of the coup, in which more than fifteen thousand persons were killed, nor the intractable durability of the military regime that followed.

At first the military government appeared to have the marks of a collegial, institutionally oriented regime with a governing junta representing the Army, Navy, Air Force, and National Police (Carabineros). As time passed, however, Pinochet's supremacy became more obvious and institutionalized, and his political skills more practiced. While drawing support from the conservative elements for his anti-Communism and free-market policies, Pinochet was able to play on the divisions among center, center-left, and left-wing parties. In two plebiscites, one of which resulted in the casuistic Constitution of 1980, Pinochet was able to command considerable, if disputed, majorities.

By the beginning of 1988, when Chile was approaching a constitutionally-mandated plebiscite on military rule, the country was no longer considered to be ruled by a collective leadership representing the various military institutions. Instead, the regime was viewed at home and abroad as Pinochet's personal vehicle. His emergence as the patrimonal ruler of Chile bears far more resemblance to the reign of Francisco Franco (whose visage on Spanish coinage was accompanied by the phrase "Caudillo by the Grace of God") than to the rotation of Brazilian and Argentine generals as chief executives of their nations.

There can be no doubt that despite Pinochet's formidable levers of patronage and coercion, his manipulative skills, and his administrative talents his power ultimately depends on his control of the military and, specifically, on his control of the Chilean Army. In any showdown among the armed forces in Chile, the Army remains decisive. For most of the twentieth century the Chilean Army has been the most professional, hierarchical, disciplined, and Prussianized military institution in Latin America.

Before Pinochet, the Chilean Army enjoyed a considerable measure of public prestige for its respect of the constitutional order and a well-earned reputation for being not only professional but also apolitical or, in the Chilean expression, "non-deliberative." This favorable image of the Army has suffered greatly under Pinochet. The decline in the military prestige has been the source of open concern among retired officers, but internal opposition to this politicization of the Army has failed to shake Pinochet's control of this military institution, just as public opposition has failed to break his domination of Chilean government.

Few persons are better equipped to analyze the political significance of Pinochet's military policies than Genaro Arriagada, whose career combines scholarship, publishing, broadcasting, and political involvement to an extent that is noteworthy even in a country known for the distinction and versatility of its intellectuals. A graduate of the law school of the University of Chile, Arriagada is president of Editorial Aconcagua, one of Chile's leading publishers, as well as head of Radio Cooperativa, an important opposition station. He has written books and articles on a variety of subjects including the Chilean landed aristocracy and military ideology in Latin America. Arriagada is also well known to scholars in the United States where he has been a Fellow of the Woodrow Wilson International Center for Scholars of the Smithsonian Institution and has lectured at the Council on Foreign Relations and at such universities as Duke, Georgetown, Columbia, and Princeton.

Arriagada is a prominent figure in the Christian Democratic Party of Chile, having served since 1975 on the party's Political Council. He headed the national campaign of opposition to the plebiscite of 1980 and was asked to play a similar role in the opposition campaign of 1988. Arriagada has also been active in organizing the peaceful demonstrations that have dramatized popular opposition to Pinochet's regime, and he will undoubtedly continue to be a key figure of the democratic opposition as the uncertain future of Chilean politics unfolds.

In *Pinochet: The Politics of Power*, Arriagada provides significant insight into the regime's internal character and the reasons for its longevity. Analyzing the mechanisms of Pinochet's control over the Chilean Army, Arriagada shows how Pinochet re-established "non-deliberation" in the Army, not in the service of a legitimate constitutional order, but at the disposition of the most personalistic dictatorship in Chilean history. At the same time, Pinochet's power over the Army's command structure has become more concentrated with the concomitant increase in his control of supposedly professional issues such as promotions and assignments.

Arriagada's remarkable account is more than a factually based analysis of the politics of a unique military regime. His study represents the informed judgment of one of Chile's leading intellectual and political figures about the means by which one man achieved control of the Chilean Army, fundamentally altering the character of a regime to place the destiny of a nation and the fate of its institutions in his own hands. No subject in the study of politics has a longer or more tragic history, and, unfortunately, no subject remains of more practical significance in contemporary world affairs.

Gilbert W. Merkx
Director
Latin American Institute
The University of New Mexico
Albuquerque, New Mexico

PART I

The Evolution of the Pinochet Regime

CHAPTER 1

The Seizure of Power

On 11 September 1973, Chile was convulsed by a violent military coup d'état. With the presidential palace besieged and in flames, President Salvador Allende committed suicide. This military takeover and Allende's sudden death shocked the world.

The coup d'état dramatically interrupted institutional life in one of the world's oldest and most stable democracies. Chilean democracy had been a noted exception to the repeated pattern of dictatorships in the developing world. For almost 150 years, the decency and civility of Chilean politics had earned the country international respect that belied its small size (a population of ten million inhabitants) and relatively weak economy.

The regime of General Augusto Pinochet that took over in 1973 remains in power today, having become one of the most enduring one-man dictatorships in the modern world. In 1988 Pinochet begins his fifteenth year of uninterrupted rule, empowered as President by means of a constitution pushed through in 1980. By 1989, when his current presidential term expires, Pinochet will have governed Chile during the administrations of five U.S. presidents: Richard Nixon, Gerald Ford, Jimmy Carter, Ronald Reagan, and Reagan's successor.

Throughout this period, international press coverage of Chile has focused on human rights and other issues of interest to world public opinion. The atrocities committed by the Pinochet regime have made Chile the object of worldwide concern. Chilean economic policies, which have rigorously followed Milton Friedman's orthodox monetarist theories, have been scrutinized by many analysts. The issue of foreign debt has also attracted outside attention because in per capita terms, Chile is the most indebted nation in the world. Meanwhile, Chile's political affairs are being monitored with growing interest by Washington—and perhaps by Moscow. More than a few analysts fear the effects of the long tenure of a right-wing dictatorship in a nation that developed the most powerful pro-Soviet Communist party in South America. Will Pinochet's legacy be a social revolution financed by parties and groups under Soviet or Cuban influence?

The Pinochet regime has obviously not been static. It has evolved through various stages and changes that will be briefly described in order to provide an introduction to the contradictory, difficult—and often fascinating—situation of one of the world's most-criticized dictatorships.

All dictatorships begin by claiming for themselves the banner of liberty, and the military officers who took power in Chile in September 1973 proved no exception. Their first public pronouncements were characterized by the term *democratic restoration*. The predominant ideological elements of this stage derived from the Chilean political traditions of democracy, respect for institutionality, and the rule of law. This first stage also evidenced a strong anti-Marxist tone and moderate economic liberalism.

The two documents that best express the ideology invoked by the government upon assuming power are Edict 5 and Decree-Law 1, which constituted the Military junta. These documents set forth the rationale used by the military to assume "the moral duty imposed by the Nation to oust a government that, although initially legitimate, fell into flagrant illegitimacy." Its illegitimacy had been "demonstrated by violations of the fundamental rights of freedom of expression, freedom of education, the right to assemble, the right to strike, the right to petition, the right to own property, and, in general, the right to a dignified and secure existence." The Allende government was further accused of having "destroyed national unity," of "neither respecting nor upholding the law," of having "acted outside the Constitution on numerous occasions," and of having failed to implement the decisions of the National Congress (Congreso Nacional), the Judiciary (Poder Judicial), and the Comptroller General of the Republic

(Contraloría General de la República). The new regime also charged the Allende government with having attempted "in a deliberate and obvious manner" to concentrate political and economic power in the executive branch, "to the detriment of vital national activities, thus gravely endangering all the rights and liberties of the inhabitants of the country."[1]

On the subject of the duration of the military regime, these documents stipulated that the Armed Forces and the National Police (Carabineros) were assuming power "only as long as circumstances so require"[2] and that they were doing so "with a patriotic commitment to restore justice, institutionality, and Chilean identity."[3] In no case was the construction of a new political and socioeconomic order presented as the task of the military.

The role of the Armed Forces in the political regime was presented as being essentially subsidiary. The military had intervened only at the last minute because it was the ultimate safeguard of the state, because it represented "the organization that the State has provided to protect itself and defend its physical and moral integrity and its historico-cultural identity."[4]

The relatively moderate tone of the early days undoubtedly reflected the search for legitimacy in the context of the political situation that preceded the coup. The principles invoked by Allende's opposition had been precisely those of liberty, democracy, autonomy of intermediate social agencies, respect for the law and the constitution, and defense of the political, economic, and social gains of the population.

During the takeover, irregular combat broke out between Chilean military forces and armed contingents of the Movimiento de Izquierda Revolutionario (MIR), an ultraleft faction with ties to Cuba, the pro-Soviet Communist party (Partido Comunista), the Socialist party (Partido Socialista), and other small leftist groups. How many died in these confrontations? The figures are contradictory, and perhaps the true number will never be known. The Inter-American Commission of Human Rights of the Organization of American States reported conservative estimates of fifteen hundred dead in the armed confrontations of 11 September 1973 and the days following, including eighty soldiers.[5]

5

Such a death toll is not inconceivable, especially considering the declarations made in the final months of the Allende government by many leaders of pro-Allende Marxist political parties. They spoke of preparations for an armed confrontation that they viewed as inevitable. It is not unreasonable, therefore, to envision an appreciable amount of resistance to the military coup.

It was clear from the beginning that the situation had gone well beyond a "confrontation" and that the military regime had initiated a practice of violating human rights that would shadow it throughout its entire history. October 1973 proved to be a month of executions. Dozens of people were assassinated: some were hastily tried by improvised Councils of War (Consejos de Guerra) and immediately shot, but most were riddled with bullets without having had the opportunity of even a rigged trial. Twenty-six persons were shot near the Chuquicamata mine in October. Elsewhere in the country, from Pisagua in the North to Valdivia in the South, at least fifty other executions were reported by the press.

Equally shocking was the continued application of the so-called fugitive law. Newspapers reported with surprising frequency attempts by leftist militants to escape from military detention centers. When they did not heed their captors' order to halt, these prisoners were killed. The extremely legalistic bureaucracy of the Chilean Armed Forces quickly provided a legal basis for this practice, as for so many others. The day after the coup, the Military Code of Justice (Código de Justicia Militar) was amended by the stipulation that "when the security of the attacked [that is, the military] so requires, the attacker or attackers may be executed in the act."[6]

In addition to human-rights problems, the difficulties of managing the economy became another major focus in the early days of the dictatorship. When the military came to power, Chile's economy was already falling apart. Major economic indicators evidenced serious imbalances in the overall economy. According to the official index, the increase in the cost of living in the twelve months preceding Allende's ouster was 304 percent. This figure, however, was fictitious. Because a substantial portion of commerce had gone underground, the inflation index could no longer measure the real cost of living. Prices were at least twice as high on the black market as they were above ground. An index compiled by the Economics Department at the University of Chile that included the effects of the black market showed that prices had risen some 647 percent between August 1972 and August 1973.

The fiscal deficit had grown so enormous that income financed only 47 percent of total expenditures of the National Treasury. Production was faltering, negatively affected by the interaction of economic, political, and social factors. A key economic factor was the deficit sustained by the businesses nationalized by the Allende government. This deficit equaled one and a half times the amount of money existing in the economy in December 1972. Among the political factors affecting industrial production were the growing wave of strikes, the constant workers' meetings and assemblies in nationalized businesses, and the besieged business atmosphere, which discouraged investment and encouraged capital flight. These serious mistakes by the Allende government had been exacerbated by financial speculation, especially in well-to-do social sectors, and by attempts to destabilize the government by aggravating the economic problems through boycotts and sabotage.

Given these conditions, the military government's economic policies had the experimental character that is common to new regimes. At first the economy was managed by a team notable for its political and ideological heterogeneity, a group not yet dominated by the orthodox monetarists who were to take over a year and a half later. Economic policy revealed more than a few inconsistencies in its objectives and policies as a result of the attempt to "satisfy the wide range of often-contradictory interests of the triumphant coalition [of the military coup], which was made up of a broad and heterogeneous spectrum of groups and classes. It included all of those who had favored the overthrow of the previous government: large and medium-sized landowners, industrial empresarios, professional schools, retail merchants, and some sectors of workers."[7]

Economic policy in this first phase reflected two major objectives. The first was to rapidly reverse the process of economic nationalization by returning to owners lands illegally occupied by peasants. This goal also entailed returning the industrial, mining, and commercial enterprises that had been taken over by Allende's government through legal maneuvering, using statutes that had been created not to carry out expropriations but to handle temporary supply problems, serious labor conflicts, or other difficulties. The second objective was to re–establish basic equilibrium in the economy at large. To this end, the government decreed a currency devaluation of some 300 percent, liberalized prices, froze salaries, and gradually reduced the fiscal deficit as well as growth of the money supply. The devaluation and the liberalization of prices reduced the inflation rate to 80 percent in the month of October 1973. This reduction, combined with fixed salaries, resulted in a sharp decrease in purchasing power.

The power structure existing in the early days was transformed strikingly in the following years. At first power was held by a military junta of equals. The commander in chief † of the Chilean Army may have even been politically disadvantaged in comparison with his counterparts in the Navy and Air Force. They had been among the instigators of the coup, while he had joined the coup plotters only at the last minute. Decree-Law 1, issued the day of the coup, explicitly asserted that the junta had assumed "Supreme Command of the Nation" with no indication that any one member held a preeminent position. On the contrary, the members of the junta were the ones who had assumed the authority to name a President. They chose "Army General Augusto Pinochet Ugarte" ‡ as President of

---

† **Translators' note:** The Chilean military term *commandante en jefe* has been literally translated as "commander in chief" (of each branch of the armed forces) reflecting the fact that this position is in the direct line of command (unlike the U.S. proximate American equivalent of "chief of staff," which is an advisory position not in the line of command.) Use of the term "commander in chief" also avoids confusion with another Chilean term "jefe de estado" or chief of staff, which is also in use. The commander in chief title as used in Chile should not be confused with the title held by the U.S. President.

‡ **Translators' note:** While in English, only the father's last name (patronym) is used, in Spanish the patronym is sometimes followed by the mother's last name (matronym). Thus Augusto Pinochet is sometimes referred to as Augusto Pinochet Ugarte.

the Junta, who will assume said post as of today."[8]

In the beginning, power seemed so evenly balanced among the commanders in chief that they apparently believed that the presidency of the junta would rotate at brief intervals. Pinochet told the press, "the Junta works as a single entity. I was elected [President of the Junta] because I am the oldest.... But I will not be the only President of the Junta; after a while, Admiral Merino will be, then General Leigh, and so on. I am not an ambitious man; I would not want to seem to be a usurper of power."[9]

Before Pinochet was selected to be President, executive power had been a function of the Military Junta as a whole. Decree Law 128 of November 1973 stated that "the Governing Junta has assumed constituent, legislative, and executive authority."[10]

The regime's public pronouncements about restoring destroyed institutionality and reestablishing democracy as rapidly as possible lasted a very short time—perhaps two weeks, at most two months. From the beginning, opinions within the regime diverged: some believed that the function of the military was to restore democracy, while others felt that its mission was to break with the past and create an entirely new political, social, economic, and military order. The second tendency ultimately prevailed, and in time, every vestige of the limited interpretation of the military's function disappeared.

Those who have studied the military mind-set agree that career officers often interpret history in terms of conspiracies and view political conflicts as categorical dilemmas. They tend to perceive genuine political differences as betrayals and to feel that the army is being stabbed in the back. Such oversimplified views led the Chilean military to believe that after the coup it would be able to rely on the gratitude and support of three important sources of power: the Catholic Church, the Western world (particularly the United States), and the democratic political parties in Chile, especially the Christian Democratic party (Democracia Cristiana). After all, their argument went, the military had intervened to prevent Allende and his allies from establishing "a New Cuba," an orthodox Socialist regime in Chile controlled and influenced by the Soviet Union.

The Chilean military had thus been part of a war against Communism, and they were succeeding.

The expected support, however, did not materialize. The extreme brutality of the military coup, the death of Salvador Allende (which, according to the evidence available to me, was not an assassination but a suicide), the bombing of the presidential palace, the executions of detainees, and the harshness of military rhetoric all combined to provoke reactions from the three sources of power that differed greatly from what the military had anticipated.

Relations between the Christian Democratic party and the military regime ruptured irremediably shortly after the military took power. The first sign of this break appeared at the celebration of Chilean Independence Day one week after the coup, when Raúl Cardinal Silva Henríquez celebrated a Te Deum. The ceremony was attended by the three living former Presidents of Chile: Gabriel González, Jorge Alessandri, and Eduardo Frei. After the ceremony, former Presidents González and Alessandri greeted the members of the Military Junta. But Christian Democratic leader Frei, shaken by the violence of the coup, refused to do so and left the church without speaking to the commanders in chief.[11] Frei subsequently declined to attend another religious ceremony of thanksgiving that the military organized in March 1974 to celebrate the first six months of the new regime. Although Eduardo Frei lived for nearly another ten years, when he died in January 1982, he had never even exchanged greetings with General Pinochet.

News of the ongoing human-rights violations galvanized in the religious community. The Catholic Church and the bishops heard many formal allegations of torture. Scarcely a month after the coup, Cardinal Silva Henríquez created the Committee of Cooperation for Peace in Chile (Comité de Cooperación para la Paz en Chile) to provide "legal, economic, technical, and spiritual assistance" to Chileans "who find themselves in serious economic or personal need due to recent political events." From this moment on, the Catholic Church assumed the defense of the human rights of those persecuted by the military regime.

These differences between the military regime and the Catholic Church and the regime and the Christian Democratic party deepened as military repression was extended throughout civil society against independent economic, cultural, and political organizations. In the aftermath of the 1973 coup, the Chilean Congress was dissolved, and a state of siege was declared that suspended individual liberties and community power. Locally elected officials were replaced in September by mayors and governors named by the Military Junta.

In October 1973, the junta took over Chilean universities and suspended all other political organizations. In November electoral rolls were nullified, and the government assumed the authority to expel persons from the country for political reasons. The junta also formally assumed constituent authority, which effectively eliminated the limits on the exercise of power that had been built into Chilean constitutional law.

In December 1973, trade unions were suspended, and the government assumed authority to remove and designate union leaders. Rules were enacted permitting the revocation of the citizenship of members of the political opposition. Emergency dispositions affecting the career stability of military officers were also mandated.

In January 1974, the resolutions concerning the suspension of non-Marxist political parties were extended. This suspension became permanent in March 1977, when the junta officially dissolved these parties and confiscated their property. The suspension of elections conducted by intermediate agencies, which had previously affected only trade unions, was extended in March 1974 to all other popular organizations, including neighborhood associations, professional schools, and community centers for mothers.

CHAPTER 2

Bases of Support

The government's pronouncements about democratic restoration rapidly changed to proposals for a genuine revolution that would create a new political, social, economic, and military order. By October 1973, government statements were already reflecting the military's new direction. The tenor of this second phase is concisely expressed in the *Declaration of Principles of the Government of Chile* (*Declaración de principios del Gobierno de Chile*), which was issued just six months after the military coup.

This document differed in tone markedly from that set in the first days of the regime. The military's term in office was no longer presented as a matter of retaining "power only as long as circumstances so require." The declaration flatly stated that "the armed forces and forces of order are not setting a fixed term for the conduct of their government because the task of moral, institutional, and material reconstruction of the country requires profound and prolonged action. In definitive terms, it is imperative to change the mentality of Chileans." The government categorically rejected the idea of "limiting itself to being a caretaker government, which would be no more than a parenthesis between two similar party-based governments." Nevertheless, the junta declared that "at an opportune time, it would hand over political power to whoever the people elect in a free, universal, secret, and informed election." The document cautioned, however, that "the foregoing does not mean that the armed forces will disengage themselves from the process of selecting the successor government or that they will observe the process as mere spectators. Quite the contrary,... [the military junta] considers part of its mission to be inspiring a great new civic and military movement...that will project the work of the present government fruitfully and enduringly into the future."[1]

Notwithstanding this open-ended commitment by the Armed Forces to governing, they henceforth viewed themselves as working within the bounds of their professional duties. The *Declaration of Principles* went on to state that when, "at an opportune time," the Governing Junta has turned over "political power to whoever the people elect,...the armed forces and forces of order will then assume the specifically institutional role of participation assigned to them by the new constitution, which will be their rightful role of safeguarding National Security, in the broad sense that said concept has at the present time."[2] The *Declaration* did not specify precisely how broad that concept might be.

During the second phase of the military takeover, the executions and applications of the "fugitive law" ceased. But the military began to employ another means of abusing human rights, that was equally or even more cruel—torture. The larger effects of torture are extraordinarily degrading to the society that suffers it and to the security forces that commit it. These effects extend to the nearly inevitably associated crime of the disappearance of persons whose arrest has been reported—the so-called arrested and disappeared (*detenidos-desaparecidos*).

Since that time, human-rights organizations have identified two distinct phases in governmental abuses of human rights in Chile. The first extended from the coup d'état through mid-1974, and the second, from mid-1974 through late 1977, when only a few exceptional cases of "arrested and disappeared" were recorded.

During the first phase, arrests were made by uniformed members of the Armed Forces or the National Police (*Carabineros*). In the second, the arrests became part of the activities of the newly-created Dirección Nacional de Inteligencia or DINA, an agency "to be equipped with an infrastructure of secret agents, unmarked vehicles, clandestine detention centers, and freedom of action for its agents."[3]

In this period, three factors dominated the Military Junta's international relations: human-rights violations, the situation of foreign refugees in Chile, and that of the Chileans who

13

had sought asylum in foreign embassies. Immediately after the coup, eight hundred foreigners, most of them refugees, requested protection from the United Nations and Christian churches. Moreover, in the days and months following the coup, thousands of Chileans crowded into foreign embassies to request asylum. How many others went into exile because of political persecution or the threat of persecution? The Inter-American Commission on Human Rights estimates that "in just the first two years of the military government, about twenty thousand Chileans left their country out of fear of political persecution."4

The protection extended by foreign embassies to those seeking asylum led to serious conflicts between the Military Junta and the governments of Sweden, France, Colombia, Venezuela, Italy, Belgium, West Germany, and Mexico. The British government recalled its ambassador to Chile because of the arrest, rape, and torture by Chilean security forces of Dr. Sheila Cassidy, a British citizen. In general, Western European countries distanced themselves from the Chilean government in the first years of the military regime. France and West Germany went further in making the extension of credit conditional upon the Junta's freeing of political prisoners.

In contrast, relations with the United States remained relatively cordial. The Nixon and Ford administrations supported the Chilean government in renegotiating its external debt with the Paris Club and other financial institutions. Economic assistance to Chile from U.S. multilateral sources during the first three years of the military regime jumped to almost ten times the amount approved during Allende's three years in office: 628 million dollars in 1974–1976, compared with 67 million in 1971–1973.

In political terms, the regime had chosen to implement a revolutionary project that clearly required excluding certain groups. The military consensus was that while the new government was eliminating the old political, social, and economic order, its representatives and institutions should be eliminated as well. This fate applied to the major political actors of the democratic period: trade unions, the entire spectrum of political parties, and any form of civilian-military relations based on the principle of civilian control. This policy of exclusion even extended to the ideologies and the mode of political behaviour that had characterized the parties of the traditional right.

What was not clear was the issue of which actors would direct and carry out this newly announced revolution. In this respect, the months of late 1974 and early 1975 were among the most decisive of the military regime.

During this period, the three fundamental bases of Pinochet's policies emerged. Notwithstanding occasional reversals and changes of direction, these bases have remained in place throughout the duration of the regime: first, the consolidation of absolute political power by the Commander in Chief of the Army; second, the unification and centralization of security forces into an all-powerful police apparatus; and third, the ascendance of a group of conservative orthodox monetarist economists who became the government's "economic team." Because many of them were graduates of the University of Chicago who followed the theories of Milton Friedman, this group came to be known as the "Chicago Boys."

In short, the structure of the military regime changed rapidly in 1974. General Pinochet, the Commander in Chief of the Army, continued to increase his power. The first and most substantial change in the power structure came with the promulgation of the Statute of the Governing Junta (Estatuto de la Junta del Gobierno). This document reiterated that executive power resided in the Military Junta and that exercise of that power was assigned to the President of the Junta. But this statute did not recognize the junta's prerogative to designate the President. Now, the presidency of the junta was to go to "the titular member who occupies the position of highest precedence in accordance with the rules established by Title IV."[5] The order of precedence could be changed only if the Commander in Chief of the Army ceased to be a member of the Military Junta, a change that could occur only through the eventualities listed in the statute: "death, resignation, or any kind of total disability of the incumbent."[6]

This statement signified that executive power had been placed in the hands of General Pinochet, who did not have a fixed term and could not be dismissed by the other members of the junta. Pinochet was invested with the title of Supreme Chief of the Nation (Jefe Supremo de la Nación), a designation that had been used in the Chilean Constitution of 1818, written immediately after independence had been won from Spain.

The statute permitted the members of the junta to retain a limited share of executive power. Junta members could "collaborate" with the Supreme Chief "in the exercise of [his] executive functions by assuming, on certain occasions, oversight of those activities, areas, and functions that he may assign them." The junta was also to have a say in the appointment—but not the dismissal—of ministers, ambassadors, intendants, and governors. The Supreme Chief would nominate these officials "with the concurrence of the Governing Junta," but the appointed officials "will retain their posts as long as they retain the confidence of the President."[7]

In what seems to have been an agreement adopted in the process of approving the statute, direction of the economy was entrusted to the commander in chief of the Navy, while the social sector was assigned to the commander in chief of the Air Force. Thus the important economic ministries of Finance (Hacienda) and Economy (Economía), as well as the Central Bank (Banco Central), were placed under the direction of Admiral José Toribio Merino, while the social ministries of Education (Educación), Housing (Vivienda), and Health (Salud) became the domain of General Gustavo Leigh. Agriculture (Agricultura) and the Ministry of Lands and Colonization (Ministerio de Tierras y Colonización) were assigned to General César Mendoza, the director general of the National Police.

Although the transfer of these functions seemed to confer enormous importance, events subsequently revealed that the dispersal of power was more apparent than real. By mid-1976, all reference to Merino and Leigh as directors of the economic and social sectors had ceased, and General Pinochet held virtually complete executive power. The *Statute of the Military Junta*, approved in June 1974, was only the beginning of a precipitous rush toward total power. In this respect, the naming of Pinochet as Supreme Chief of the Nation proved to be a transitional step.

Exactly six months after the *Statute of the Junta* was enunciated, a new decree introduced a small but significant modification: Pinochet's title of Supreme Chief of the Nation was changed to President of the Republic, the traditional designation of Chilean chiefs of state. The new decree stated, "Executive power is exercised by the President of the Governing Junta, who, with the title of President of the Republic of Chile, administers the State and is the Supreme Chief of the Nation."[8]

In formal terms, this modification was a minor change that had only limited legal importance. Its greatest significance was political. The change in title represented an attempt to shore up the doubtful legitimacy and transitory character of the authoritarian regime by endowing it with the solemnity and stability that had always been associated with the presidency of the republic. This new designation also distanced the President further from the other members of the Military Junta in the pyramid of power.

Pinochet's personal political power, however, was just one of the pillars on which the regime was being constructed. The second was to be the police. The existing situation was a complex one. Since the day of the coup, the intelligence services in all branches of the Armed Forces had expanded enormously and become far more active. Because of the rivalry among intelligence services, the repressive power of the state was fragmenting into a multitude of agencies that were increasingly difficult to control. This decentralizing trend aggravated a tendency toward legal and political irresponsibility. By late 1973 and the first half of 1974, it had become enormously difficult to determine the whereabouts of political detainees and to identify which intelligence service had arrested them. The Ministry of Interior was apparently responsible only for the civil police. Each branch of the military—and even the National Police—had its own institutional police services that answered only to its respective commander in chief. It became common for individuals who had been arrested, interrogated, and released to be immediately arrested again by a different police service.

The creation of DINA in June 1974, put an end to such occurrences. From this point on, intelligence activity was entrusted to a single "military agency of a technical-professional nature, answering directly to the Governing Junta." [9] DINA was supposed to include personnel from all branches of the defence establishment, as well as civilians hired for special purposes. In actuality, the establishment of DINA was not an administrative or bureaucratic measure. DINA emerged as the legal and institutional manifestation of the victory of the Army's security apparatus over all the others. From June 1974 on, security functions—the backbone of any police state—were in the hands of the Army. The Navy and Air Force were quickly "returned to barracks" and the National Police were assigned a subordinate role in handling minor tasks.

Although DINA had been created to give the Military Junta complete control of police power, subsequent events showed that police power was exercised solely by the Supreme Chief of the Nation. The degree to which Pinochet dominated DINA was emphasized by General Gustavo Leigh, commander in chief of the Air Force, years after his removal from the Military Junta:

> I was constantly recalling [Air Force personnel] from DINA, but do not believe that it was because they were doing unsavory things. Rather, it was because of the absolute preeminence of the Army in DINA. They requested personnel from all branches, but it turned out that the officers who we sent to DINA were not given any executive work, only administrative jobs. In practice, the organization was directly subordinate to the President, although legally it was supposed to be subordinate to the Governing Junta. So I pulled my people when I realized that I had no power over DINA. [10]

It would be difficult to exaggerate the degree to which control of DINA concentrated power in the hands of the Chief of State. From mid-1974 until it was dissolved in August 1977, DINA was the backbone of the regime; during this period, no agency in Chile had greater impact on national life. The President's absolute authority over DINA effectively dispelled any pretense of equality between him and those who, in the months immediately following the coup, had been his peers.

The third pillar of the regime began to be erected when the "Chicago Boys" took over the military government's economic team. The group that had managed the economy during the first year of the military government had not succeeded in controlling the dizzying price increases. Anti-inflationary policies had reduced inflation from 600 percent to 350 percent in the first year, but prices began to rise again in October 1974. In November 1974, the inflation rate began an increase that continued into the following months. By March 1975, inflation had reached a rate of 20 percent per month. This trend was doubly worrisome because of a simultaneous reduction in the rate of growth of the money supply.

This crisis split the upper levels of the economic hierarchy, and from this schism, a group of orthodox monetarist economists emerged victorious. These right-wing economists were ideologically tied to Milton Friedman, the University of Chicago professor and 1976 Nobel laureate. Some members of the group had earned postgraduate degrees at Chicago, and their ties to Friedman surfaced immediately before the ministerial crisis precipitating the change in economic policy that consolidated their power. In late March 1975, Professor Friedman arrived in Chile, having been invited by the Foundation of Economic Studies (Fundación de Estudios Económicos) of the Mortgage Development Bank of Chile (Banco Hipotecario de Fomento de Chile), one of the two main financial groups at that time. Friedman made several presentations, the most important being a public address at the headquarters of the Military Junta on 26 March 1975.

"I believe," he stated, "that Chile has two basic problems today: the first, very obvious one, is controlling inflation; the second is establishing a vigorous market economy." He then jumped into the debate that had divided the shaky alliance determining economic policy. The debate centered on whether inflation should be dealt with by gradual measures or by "shock treatment." "I do not think that a gradualist policy makes sense in Chile," said Friedman. "I am afraid that the patient might die before the treatment takes effect. I think Chile has much to gain by examining

19

examples of 'shock treatment' for the problems of inflation and disorganization."[11]

Encouraged by their teacher, the "Chicago Boys" launched their "decisive battle" for control of key economic posts. On 17 April 1975, Jorge Cauas and Sergio de Castro became the heads of the government's economic team as the ministers of Finance and Economy, respectively. Pablo Barahona became the president of the Central Bank (Chile's Federal Reserve bank) and Alvaro Bardón became its vice-president. Castro was the undisputed leader of the group of economists, and Barahona and Bardón were among its key opinion leaders. When he took charge of the economic team, Jorge Cauas announced an "economic shock" policy intended to control inflation and privatize the economy, beginning with the banks that were until then controlled mainly by the state.

The "Chicago Boys" became the third pillar of support for Pinochet's regime for a long time. They arrived on the scene in a curious fashion, however. It was not Pinochet who instigated their entrance but the Navy commander in chief, Admiral Merino. At the time, Pinochet was evidently too busy establishing control over the Military Junta and the Army. As previously noted, Merino had been assigned control of the economic ministries early on, when executive power was shared, and the Navy continued to control economic matters after reform of the *Statute of the Military Junta* turned executive power over to Pinochet. As it turned out, the effect of the shock treatment was so dramatic and its social cost so enormous that no individual, no branch of the Armed Forces, nor any member of the Military Junta wanted to claim responsibility for the decisions of the technocrats.

CHAPTER 3

The Crisis of 1975

In 1975 the Chilean gross domestic product fell 13 percent, and unemployment reached 20 percent of the work force, four times the historic mean. Public investment fell by half, while the interest rate rose to the unprecedented level of 23 percent. The annual inflation rate reached 343 percent, surpassing 300 percent for the third consecutive year.

The country was dragged into a catastrophic recession. The unemployed filled the streets, hundreds of industries were paralyzed, and hunger reigned in the poor neighborhoods. Under these conditions, the internal political opposition unleashed an offensive against the regime. Thousands of copies of *El Mandato de la historia y las exigencias del porvenir* (The Mandate of History and the Demands of the Future), a short book by former President Eduardo Frei, circulated clandestinely. In it Frei attacked the government for violating human rights, depriving Chileans of political freedom and trade-union activities, precipitating a deterioration in international relations, and imposing an economic policy that he judged to be not only technically incorrect but one that exacted an unnecessarily high social cost.

Amidst this crisis, the regime accentuated the military component of its ideology. The regime's rhetoric became openly dominated by two central precepts of military ideology: the doctrine of counterinsurgency warfare and elements of geopolitical thought found in a particular version of national security doctrine. The regime's ideology thus merged with military ideology into a seamless whole.

Yet this preeminence of elements central to military ideology did not result from any surprising turnabout; these elements had been present since the regime took power

21

and had figured prominently in the *Declaration of Principles*. Almost two years later, the government disseminated the document entitled *National Objective of the Government of Chile* (*Objectivo Nacional del Gobierno de Chile*), which was based on the concept of national security, conditioned by economic liberalism.[1]

An ideological definition was thus taking shape. It was best articulated in the Presidential Messages (Mensajes Presidenciales) of 1975 and 1976 and in the clauses and resolutions of Constitutional Acts 2, 3 and 4. In 1976, the third year after the coup, the doctrines of national security and counterinsurgency achieved unchallenged dominance.

The military regime's vision of its mission and tenure grew out of the war against communism, and the enemy was clearly Marxism. According to Pinochet, "Marxism is an intrinsically perverse doctrine, and everything that springs from it, as healthy as it might appear, is consumed by the poison that corrodes its roots. This is the meaning of the statement that its error is intrinsic, and therefore global in the sense that no dialogue or transaction is compatible with it." Such was the ideological significance of Marxism; in practice it took the form of "a permanent aggression, today in the service of Soviet imperialism.... [T]his modern form of permanent aggression gives rise to an unconventional war, in which territorial invasion is replaced by the attempt to control countries from within."[2]

This conception of war defined the role and duration of Chile's military government. The definition could hardly be broader: "Another product of the preceding analysis is the understanding that power must be vested in the Armed Forces and the Forces of Order, since only they have the organization and the means to confront Marxism transformed into permanent aggression."[3]

This anticommunist "war" demanded categorical rejection of the liberal state. General Pinochet announced in his 1976 Presidential Message that "Chile has ceased to be an ideologically neutral state, as was advocated by philosophical liberalism, and has resolutely adopted a clear, solid, and vigorous doctrine." Four months later, in January 1977, Admiral Merino was equally emphatic:

22

Let us put it realistically: the world today has one enemy—communism. A monolithic, impenetrable enemy that has acquired technology as good as that of the democratic system but used exclusively for destruction. And it is attempting to dominate the entire world. So, what system should be chosen to combat this monolithic bandit that does not show its face, whose religion is the lie? Only war, I do not doubt that, and before the end of this century. And what possibility do we have of surviving a war, if the Congress of the United States, which is the country best equipped to fight it, calls on a general or an admiral and has him reveal to the whole world the U.S. strategy for attacking Russia? It's insane.

Merino was then asked, "In that case, if the only means of interaction is war, can there be only military governments?" The admiral responded, "What other way is there? Which way? How?"[4]

This manner of thinking brings to mind the theories of total war of General Erich von Ludendorff. According to his view, war is total in many senses. It is total in time because it has no end. Everything is war because there is no point in distinguishing between periods of war and peace. This war involves every country but has neither borders nor national differences because the enemy is simultaneously internal and external. It is a total war in the variety of its means—armed, economic, psychosocial, and, only in the last instance, military. The inevitable corollary of this apocalyptic vision is that "power must be vested in the armed forces" permanently because the agression that threatens to destroy the state is permanent. According to this scheme of things, there is undoubtedly no role for the people, no prospect for democracy.

Even more seriously, analyses of the period and studies of Chilean, Argentine, Uruguayan, and Brazilian military ideologies indicate that this concept of antisubversive war entails a military theory that legitimates violence and torture.[5] The ideas found in speeches and articles and even in the reasoning behind the sentence in an important military trial all indicate that the concept of a war against subversion is similar or identical to the so-called "French antisubversive doctrine" developed by a group of French Army officers during the wars in Vietnam (1945–1954) and Algeria (1954–1962).[6]

Communists are viewed by the Pinochet regime as animals who are practically inhuman, the source of "murderous ideas."[7] A Chilean colonel speaking at the Institute of Political Science (Instituto de Ciencias Políticas) of the Catholic University in 1976 asserted that communism "utilizes any pressure or action to achieve its ends. It is by its choice of tactics that communism demonstrates its total moral debility: blackmail, terrorism, vandalism, genocide, crimes against the state, degradation, vilification, drugs, depravation."[8] "Communism," said Pinochet, "promotes all types of disorder. Material disorder through street agitations. Economic disorder through demagogic and inflationary pressures. Social disorder through constant strikes. Moral disorder by encouraging drugs, pornography, family divisions. Spiritual disorder through systematic class hatred. And as an aberrant synthesis of all of these, terrorism arises and spreads."[9]

According to this simplistic conception, subversion is not perceived as exclusively or even predominantly a political problem. It is a problem of evil and weakness in human nature in which good and bad are absolutely distinct. Marxism is not only "intrinsically perverse," but its supporters are completely corrupted beings who lack scruples, ethics, and morality. Is there any need, then, to be concerned about the means used in this dirty and endless war? Is torture forbidden if it is the price of saving Western Christian culture?

Roger Trinquier, a French officer known for his defense of this notion of a war against subversion, offers his views in a book that was translated into Spanish and circulated widely among the armies of Southern South America: "[T]he terrorist has become a soldier, as have the aviator and the gunner," and in war there is a special poison for every soldier. Thus the aviator is destroyed by the antiaircraft battery and the infantry soldier by gunfire. But what is the special poison for the terrorist? Trinquier names it obliquely: "If the prisoner quickly provides the information asked for, the interrogation ceases. But if this information is not produced immediately, his adversaries are forced to obtain it by any means necessary."[10]

This ideological framework corresponded to an extremely harsh period of the regime that was expressed in sweeping human-rights violations and severe restrictions on freedom of the press.[11] The distinctive characteristic of human-rights violations in 1975 and 1976 was the disappearance of persons who had been arrested. The Catholic Church's humanitarian organization, the Vicariate of Solidarity (Vicaría de la Solidaridad), kept statistics on these cases. The Vicariate recorded 668 cases of persons whose arrests were reported and verified, and who then disappeared. They were never heard from again, nor were their bodies ever found. In 1975 there were 75 cases of "arrested and disappeared"; the following year, there were 109.

With respect to these disappearances, the Inter-American Commission on Human Rights said in its 1985 report: "[N]ew evidence shows that three basic methods were used to eliminate the disappeared: some were drugged and then thrown from helicopters into the sea, others were burned and buried in the vicinity of Peldehue, and others were killed and thrown in the Cajón del Maipo."[12]

Torture was another aberrant reality during this period. The Inter-American Commission on Human Rights noted that in the Pinochet regime, "the practice of torture has been neither the result of individual excesses committed by members of security agencies nor a phenomenon tolerated out of indifference or weakness by other Chilean institutions; on the contrary, torture has been and continues to be a deliberate policy of the Chilean government carried out during the entire period that began on 11 September 1973."[13]

Although the ideological discourse of this stage was too extreme to last, the central elements of its rationale have been present throughout the history of the regime. They have diminished in intensity during periods of lessened repression but have reappeared with increased harshness at times when Pinochet and his government have felt challenged and have established a harder line in response to perceived threats.

The component of the so-called national security doctrine that has survived in the long run—and even gained influence over time—has been anticommunism. The theme of anti-communism is part of the Pinochet regime and of the rhetoric of the Chief of State, where it has recurred like an endless monologue. More than ten years after the 1976 Presidential Message just cited, Pinochet was still stressing the theme of anticommunism.

CHAPTER 4

The Chilean "Economic Miracle"

The first stirrings of the economic "boom" were felt in 1977. The Chilean "economic miracle" took center stage not only economically but politically and socially as well. The gross domestic product (GDP), having fallen 12.9 percent in 1975, recovered 3.5 percent in 1976. In 1977 Chile enjoyed a spectacular growth rate of 9.9 percent, the highest in several decades. This notable growth continued in 1978 and 1979, when production increased 8.2 percent and 8.3 percent respectively. In 1980, however, the growth rate declined moderately to 6.5 percent.

These conditions allowed the neoconservative technocrats who had taken control of the Chilean economy to consolidate their power and, allied with like-minded civilians, to extend this control into many realms of national life. Integrating civilians into a government as markedly military as Pinochet's, however, presented more than a few difficulties. Generally speaking, two kinds of civilian participation in the Chilean Cabinet have evolved. Some civilians have participated as isolated individuals, contributing their abilities and personal viewpoints for as long as required. Others have come into government as part of a "team" that could counterbalance certain tendencies of the military and offer a particular project to the military regime.

The individual kind of civilian integration is not significant. It can best be described as "co-operation," a process in which some individuals are absorbed by the institutions, projects, and values of the dominant group, in this case the Armed Forces.

The second form of integration, in contrast, is highly significant. Civilian groups bring a set of ideas and projects as well as a different mentality and style to a common political enterprise that then ceases to be defined as purely military and becomes "civilian-military." The proper description of this second form of integration would be "participation." In such cases, the civilian team contributes something that the military makes its own, and in exchange, the military offers other ideas, criteria, and projects that the civilian team accepts as its own.

The only years when the Pinochet government could be called a civilian-military regime were those between 1976–1981. During that period, the military accepted a civilian group's project of social transformation that amounted to a conservative counterrevolution.

In December 1976, when Jorge Cauas resigned from the Ministry of Finance, the "Chicago Boys" took total control of the country's economy. At that time, a reshuffling occurred that was characteristic of a highly integrated team solidly in power. Minister of Economy Sergio de Castro took over the principal ministry, that of Finance. The president of the Central Bank (Pablo Barahona) was appointed minister of economy. The vice-president of the Central Bank (Alvaro Bardón) assumed the bank's presidency, while the third-highest executive of the bank (Sergio De la Cuadra) took over its vice-presidency.

The alliance that eventually attained maximum civilian participation in government policy-making was put together during 1977. This alliance achieved complete sway in April 1978, when Pinochet named Comptroller General of the Republic Sergio Fernández as minister of interior. Fernández was the first civilian (and the only one during the first ten years of the military regime) to hold the post of minister of interior. He declared to the press, "My nomination suits the objective of achieving maximum civilian integration into the Cabinet," and he effectively achieved this goal. The Cabinet proposed by Fernández and accepted by the President consisted of twelve civilians and only five military officers.

This group of civilians shared common ideas about what should be done regarding Chile's economy, politics, and international relations. Never questioning their own loyalty to the authoritarian regime and to Pinochet, they offered their "Program of Government" (Programa de Gobierno). In political terms, the watchword of their program was *institutionalization*. In economic matters they supported the neoconservative model inspired by the ideas of Milton Friedman. In international affairs, they proposed opening Chile to international financial circles, seeking reapproachment with the United States, and improving the regime's image abroad.

The ideological discourse of the economic miracle was as adamant about the country's economic past as it was optimistic about the future. Chile was described as having been through decades of a process of deterioration "resulting from years of demagogy and erroneous economic policies" that were the consequence of excessive state involvement, excessive trade protection that had guaranteed utility monopolies, and economic measures that had protected business and trade-union minorities to the serious detriment of consumers.

For the future, the new economic team promised unheard-of levels of economic development. By means of a policy of extreme economic liberalism, Chile would replicate the developmental feats of West Germany and Japan after World War II, or of Taiwan, Singapore, and South Korea in more recent years. This extremely optimistic projection, which time would prove hasty and unfounded, was not only maintained by the press and the government propaganda apparatus but was dressed in "scientific" clothing and taught in Chilean universities. In May 1977, José Piñera, an economist who later became a prominent government minister, described the "economic miracle" in these terms:

> The profound economic transformation that has taken place in Chile makes it impossible to utilize econometric models based on the parameters of the past to project the future. Although we are aware of the fragility [of any projection], we have constructed a tentative and heterodox exercise in projection.... The conclusion is that the country can grow at an average annual rate of 8 percent from 1981 to 1990 and achieve the potential gross domestic product of a nation such as ours. From

then on, it is possible to foresee a "normal" growth rate of 6 percent per year. Consequently, and if an annual growth rate of 5.5 percent is expected through 1980, the average growth rate for the rest of the century would be 7 percent annually.... [I]f these projections are realized, in 1984 we will recuperate the gross domestic product that we would have achieved if we had maintained the historic growth rate since 1970. The country will double its 1976 gross domestic product (GDP) in ten years instead of nineteen, as it would have done at the historic rate, and will double the 1976 per capita GDP in fourteen years instead of forty-one. In the year 2000, Chile will have a total GDP of 42,500 million dollars, similar to the present GDP of Belgium, and a per capita GDP of 2,200 dollars. [1]

The sense of witnessing an "economic miracle" was widely shared by many sectors of the Chilean business world, especially the largest businesses. Yet their enthusiastic adherence to the model promoted by the "Chicago Boys" was surprising because the resulting economic policy was severely damaging the structure of production, especially in industry, agriculture, and mining. Sharp reduction of import tariffs and the substantial opening of the economy to foreign commerce left the main domestic producers unprotected from foreign competition. At the same time, high interest rates were creating business indebtedness to the banking system that could only be masked by the continuous influx of new credits. These new credits aggravated the situation, producing a pyramid of debts that were continually being increased by the capitalization of interest. In 1979 exchange rates were frozen, which exacerbated the lack of protection for Chilean industry, created an even more powerful stimulus for imports, and further weakened the competitiveness of Chilean products in foreign markets.

But that was just one side of the coin. The other was that the policies of the "Chicago Boys" had stimulated one of the most accelerated processes of concentration of economic power in South America in decades. A study based on available data for late 1978 showed that five large financial conglomerates controlled 36 percent of the 250 largest Chilean enterprises, along with 53 percent of their capital. The 214 domestically owned private businesses were managed by only 80 individuals.[2]

This high degree of concentration had occurred fundamentally through brazen (and irresponsible, as later events would demonstrate) manipulation of the capital market. The large financial groups had used the opening to external financial markets to create "economic empires" that were huge in proportion to the size of the Chilean economy. These empires suffered from an intrinsic weakness: only a small part of their borrowing was earmarked for investment, as was evidenced by the low investment rates of those years. The foreign credits, most of them private foreign loans without government backing, were used to buy assets and businesses from the state or from weaker private businesses, to accumulate capital, and to make enormous profits by appropriating the differential between the interest rates paid to international private banks and the higher interest rates at which these monies were loaned on the domestic market.[3]

Chile's "economic miracle" began during a serious crisis in the country's international relations, particularly with the United States. On 21 September 1976, a car bomb exploded in Washington, D.C., killing Orlando Letelier, a Chilean exile who had been President Allende's foreign minister. Also killed was Ronni Moffit, a U.S. citizen working as an aide to Letelier.

Investigations by the Washington prosecutor, the FBI, and other U.S. agencies determined that DINA, the Chilean secret police, had participated in the bombing. A District of Columbia grand jury charged Michael Townley, a U.S. citizen working for DINA, with the killings. Also accused were several Chileans, including the head of DINA, General Manuel Contreras Sepúlveda, Army Colonel Pedro Espinoza, one of Contreras's closest and most influential collaborators, and Armando Fernández Larios, a young Army captain.[4] At that time, General Contreras was the second-most-powerful individual in Chile and a close friend of Pinochet and his family.

This appalling crime was followed by another event that was a setback for Pinochet: the election of Jimmy Carter as President of the United States. When President Carter subsequently made defense of human rights a cornerstone of his foreign policy, relations between Chile and the United States reached an all-time low. As Heraldo Muñoz has observed, "The Carter administration voted in international organizations to condemn the Chilean government's human-rights procedures; it officially received opposition leaders such as Eduardo Frei and Clodomiro Almeyda; and it pressured the military regime to improve the human-rights situation in Chile."[5] The Carter administration's concern with human rights in Chile also led to sanctions and other pressures against Pinochet. For example, in 1976 the U.S. Congress terminated all new programs of military assistance and arms sales to the Chilean government.

Chile's international difficulties thus created serious roadblocks for the technocrats who were attempting to implement the promised "economic miracle." They needed an opening of foreign financial markets and wanted to attract some of the resources accumulated from increases in the world price of oil. Piñera said, "There has occurred an increase in world savings, leading fluid capital to seek countries with stable economic and political situations. The uncertain situation in most of the rest of the developing world provides some Latin American countries, especially Chile, with the opportunity to use these resources in its development process."[6]

Because Chile had a stable authoritarian regime and extremely liberal economic policies, its private conglomerates and businesses were being presented in those years as ideal loan recipients. Thus began Chile's frenzied accumulation of one of the world's highest foreign debts per capita.

The country could not be opened to international financial markets without changes in the critical areas of human and political rights. Multiple pressures forced the Pinochet regime to abandon the "language of war" that had characterized its pronouncements in 1975 and 1976. These factors included the economic situation, domestic opposition, forces that were lobbying within the government to open the country to international financial markets, the Carter administration's focus on human rights, and the need to alleviate U.S. pressure concerning the Letelier-Moffit case. The combined pressures led the Pinochet regime to commit itself to a moderate political opening whose two main components were the dissolution of DINA and the proposals enunciated in the Chacarillas Address (Discurso de Chacarillas).

In August 1977, U.S. Assistant Secretary of State for Inter-American Affairs Terence Todman visited Chile. During his stay, the Chilean government dissolved DINA and created the National Information Center (Centro Nacional de Informaciones or CNI) to replace it. This change appeared to be minor in legal terms as was evidenced by the similarity of the decrees establishing DINA and the CNI. But the change was well received within and beyond Chile because DINA had become one of the most servile secret police agencies in the world. Its founder, General Manuel Contreras Sepúlveda, was sent into retirement, an event that marked the exit of one of Pinochet's closest associates and one of the men most hated and feared by Chileans.

On 9 July 1977, one month before DINA was dissolved, Pinochet gave the so-called Chacarillas Address, which included a lukewarm announcement of a democratization process and proposed a timetable for institutionalizing the regime and normalizing the political process. This proposal certainly represented progress, although it was perhaps less than impressive, considering that full democracy was not scheduled to be achieved until 1991, fourteen years after the announcement of the "democratization plan."

The Chacarillas Address outlined three stages of democratization. During the first stage, which was to end by 31 December 1980, power was to be held entirely by the Armed Forces, with civilian collaboration. In the second stage, which was to last five years (until 31 December 1985), power would be shared by the Armed Forces and civilians. General Pinochet would continue as President and the Military Junta would retain some of its legislative functions, although its powers would be reduced. A civilian legislative chamber would be created but its members were to be selected not by universal suffrage but by the Governing Junta. The last stage of normalization would begin by 31 December

1985. At that time, the legislative chamber would elect a President, and a new constitution would be promulgated. During this stage, power would be exercised directly and predominantly by civilians.

Unlike the 1976 proposal, the Chacarillas Address assigned a curiously ambigious political role to the military. Pinochet spoke of a "security force" whose dimensions and scope would be defined by the Commission of Constitutional Reform (Comisión de Reforma Constitucional) and more concretely by the new constitution. "As an integral part of an authoritarian democracy," Pinochet said in 1977, "it will be necessary to reserve for the institutions of National Defense that judicial participation required by their function as a future security force, which, rising above political contingencies, must be structured to represent what is most permanent in the nation and to exercise the protective function demanded by its character."[7] This entire procedure was to lead eventually to a democratic order that could be described as authoritarian, protected and integrating, technocratic, and authentically participatory.

In retrospect, it is clear that this promise of a political opening was part of a political strategy intended to alleviate U.S. pressure over the Letelier case. Pinochet personally orchestrated the signals of progress toward a democracy that was never to materialize. In April 1978, General Enrique Montero, the Chilean subsecretary (vice-minister) of interior, signed an agreement with Earl Silbert, the U.S. Attorney for the District of Columbia, in which the Pinochet regime committed itself to full collaboration in the investigation of the Letelier-Moffit killings. Subsequent events, however, particularly statements made eight years later in January 1987 by Captain Fernández Larios to a U.S. court, showed that the Chilean government did not abide by the agreement.[8] A complete cover-up operation was assembled under Pinochet's direction with the active participation of top army officials and General Contreras. The cover-up successfully hid the participation of the Chilean military in the terrorist act and thus closed the door on the U.S. investigation.

On 13 May 1979, the Chilean Supreme Court (Corte Suprema)—an entity that the Chilean opposition consistently accuses of working with the dictatorship—refused to extradite General Contreras, Colonel Espinoza, and Captain Fernández to the United States. State Department spokesperson Hodding Carter declared: "We are deeply disappointed by the decision of the President of the Chilean Supreme Court yesterday in the Letelier-Moffit assassination case.... The evidence submitted by the United States to the Chilean Supreme Court was clearly sufficient to support the accusation. The strength of this evidence was confirmed on 14 February 1979 by the jury of this city [Washington, D.C.] that indicted two other suspects in this case.... We do not believe that yesterday's decision is in accord with international judicial standards."[9]

Following this decision by the Chilean Supreme Court, the U.S. government recalled its ambassador to Chile, George Landau, to discuss the Letelier case. A career diplomat committed to the cause of human rights, Landau had earned international respect by opening the U.S. embassy to a wide array of social and political groups, including union leaders and the democratic opposition. A short time later, again because of the Letelier case, the Carter administration approved new sanctions against the Chilean government. In November 1979, personnel at the Chilean diplomatic mission were reduced by some 25 percent. All sales of weapons parts were terminated, and the U.S. military mission in Santiago was ended. Also, loans from the Export-Import Bank to the Pinochet government were prohibited as were activities by the Overseas Private Investment Corporation (OPIC) in Chile. Finally, in early 1980, the U.S. government chose not to invite the Chilean Navy to participate in the twenty-first Operation Unitas (a U.S.–sponsored hemispheric naval exercise).

But these sanctions produced no political effects. The generous flow of loans from U.S. banks to private Chilean economic groups more than compensated for what the U.S. government was denying the Chilean regime. It was commonly said in those days that the poor relations between Chile and the Carter administration were neutralized by the good relations between the Chilean financial sector and U.S. private banks. Pinochet was said to have told his inner circle that "the rejection of the White House and Capitol Hill does not matter as long as my government gets along well with Wall Street." Chilean Air Force Commander in Chief General Fernando Matthei expressed the same idea in a more sophisticated way: "Our relationship with the United States armed forces is very good. Our relationship with the State Department is very bad. But our relationship with economic circles is excellent."[10]

In actuality, the Letelier case and Chile's poor relationship with the Carter administration could not dampen the enthusiasm brought about by the "economic miracle." Thus fortified by his alliance with the civilians who directed the major ministries and the private economic sector, Pinochet took several more steps toward acquiring total power. Accession to the presidency in 1974 had already provided him with the greatest concentration of personal power seen in Chile in the twentieth century. But his power in one area did not equal that of his democratically elected predecessors. Ironically, this area was the military realm.

Within the Army, his own branch of the military, General Pinochet's authority has been enormous and unchecked since 11 September 1973. Such a degree of unregulated power, particularly over officers' careers, would be inconceivable in a democratic government. In the other branches of the military, however, President Pinochet lacks the authority to name or retire the commanders in chief, a power previously exercised by Chile's constitutional Presidents.

This limitation on the power of the reformulated presidency became increasingly apparent as differences developed between Pinochet and General Leigh, the commander in chief of the Air Force. When a legal solution proved to be unattainable, the struggle between the two junta members was finally resolved by means of a power play. The *Statute of the Governing Junta* had defined the positions of commander in chief and junta member as lifetime posts that could be forfeited only through "death, resignation, or any kind of total disability of the incumbent." But General Leigh did not want to resign, and he enjoyed good health. Nevertheless, on 24 July 1978, Leigh's dismissal was announced in a supreme decree (*decreto supremo*) by the Ministry of Interior. The document declared that the Air Force general would be unable to continue as a member of the Governing Junta due to "total disability."

This decree ran roughshod over official policy because the "total disability" referred to in the law could only be psychological or physical. In no case could political differences, however profound, be understood as such. Nonetheless, so-called total disability was used as a legal loophole to dismiss a junta member for political reasons. This end was achieved by means of an article of the *Statute of the Governing Junta* that states: "In case of uncertainty about whether the disability that prevents a member of the Governing Junta from exercising his duties is of such a nature as to require his replacement,... it will fall to the titular members of the Junta to decide the matter."[11]

On the morning of 24 July 1978, the other three members of the Military Junta had declared that Leigh was "totally unable to continue performing his duties." This declaration was made in an internal memo that neither Leigh nor the nation has yet seen. Armed with this allegation, President Pinochet and the minister of interior dictated a decree dismissing the third-ranking member of the junta. The comptroller general of the republic, who is responsible for reviewing the legality of supreme decrees, approved this document with the surprising interpretation that "said act legally constitutes a decree law and not a supreme decree."

What is important here, however, is not legality but power. General Leigh's dismissal was the decisive step that undid the balance of power between the Military Junta and the commander in chief of the Army.

From that moment on, General Pinochet began to act as the de facto, if not the de jure, Generalissimo of the Armed Forces. In September 1979, Pinochet used the title for the first time in his annual Presidential Message: "The high commanders are responsible for informing their subordinates about matters of government, an obligation that has been assumed by the President of the Republic, in his capacity as Generalissimo of the Armed Forces and Forces of Order."[12]

Throughout 1979 General Pinochet consistently differentiated between himself as President and the other members of the Military Junta, particularly at official ceremonies. On

21 May at the centennial celebration of the Naval Battle of Iquique (Combate Naval de Iquique) and at the observance of the birthday of Chilean independence hero Bernardo O'Higgins on 20 August, five floral offerings were presented in an order that conveyed a symbolic message. The first offering came from the President of the Republic and was placed by Pinochet and his minister of defense. The second, from the Chilean Army, was placed by the vice-commander in chief and the chief of staff of the Army. The third, fourth, and fifth, representing the Navy, the Air Force, and the National Police (Carabineros), were placed by the corresponding members of the Governing Junta accompanied by one general from each branch. Thus protocol in military ceremonies pointed to the existence of a presidential power above the commanders in chief of the military (represented by the vice-commander in chief in the case of the Army), emphasizing in this manner the authority of the Generalissimo of the Armed Forces.

Once he had ousted General Leigh from the junta, Pinochet redefined the political role of the military. In his 1979 Presidential Message, the Armed Forces were excluded from any significant political participation for the first time, and the traditional concept of military professionalism was stressed. At first glance, the speech seemed to revalidate the Armed Forces' traditional democratic principles of professionalism, subordination to political power, nonintervention in politics, and political neutrality: "It also gives us great satisfaction to state that our Armed Forces and Forces of Order have not been politicized, as they have understood that the functions of the state rest with their Commanders in Chief and General Director respectively." Pinochet stressed that these leaders alone are responsible for governing. The role of the others, from generals to vice-admirals to the troops, is not to engage in political deliberation but to receive direct reports on these subjects from their commanders in chief. Pinochet emphasized:

The high officers are responsible for informing their subordinates about matters of government, an obligation that the President of the Republic himself has assumed...to inform not only the officers but all garrisons about the national situation and actions of the Government. But all this should be done without ever falling into political deliberation, which has caused the erosion of unity and prestige when some military governments, in other countries as well as in our own history, have slid into this error. [Avoiding political involvement] has allowed the armed forces of our National Defense to maintain optimum professionalism and preparedness.[13]

CHAPTER 5

Seeking Legitimacy

The year 1980 was a euphoric one for the regime. Never before or since has an environment of such confidence existed in Chile. The growth of the GDP in 1980 reached a high of 6.5 percent. That was to be the last year of the economic miracle, which twelve months later would burst like a bubble. But 1980 was also a year of incautious optimism. The arrogance of those managing the economy during that period reached a level that in hindsight appears both pathetic and ridiculous.

Sergio de Castro, the minister of finance and the indisputable leader of the "Chicago Boys," affirmed in May 1980 that "the economy is growing in such a way that in eleven years, per capita income could double, while in the past this [doubling] was only achieved in forty-six years."[1] He promised that by the end of the 1980s, when the pending economic plans were completed, Chile would be "a developed country with a per capita gross domestic product of thirty-five hundred dollars annually," raising it above the global average.[2] "In 1990," promised José Piñera, then minister of labor (Trabajo), "Chile will be a developed country.... In 1990 this country will have surpassed the average global per capita income, which is approximately eighteen hundred dollars. That is, at the end of the [transition] period that the constitution projects for the President, at that moment the military government and the Chilean people will have transformed a destroyed Chile into a developed country."[3]

Indeed, Chile was enjoying an atmosphere of great prosperity. Much later (and too late), this prosperity would be revealed to have been fictitious wealth, but at the time, few slowed down long enough to analyze the situation. Meanwhile, the Chilean foreign debt was growing at a tremendous rate. The year 1977 was the last that this debt showed a relatively moderate increase, 481 million dollars. In 1978 the figure rose to 1.46 billion; in 1979 new loans increased to 1.82 billion; and in 1980, they reached 2.6 billion dollars.

Equally significant was the composition of the foreign debt. Of the 10.37 billion dollars of new credits advanced between 1977 and 1980, 84 percent were private-sector loans from international banks.[4] But the most unusual feature of these large credits was the manner in which they were used. In other countries, foreign borrowing has served as the basis for increased investment and, by this route, what could be termed as process of debt-financed economic growth. But in Chile, a substantial portion of the foreign credit was used to finance consumption. There occurred "a deficit in current accounts promoted by the debt, with a negative impact on national production, derived from flooding the domestic market with imports and the reduction of exports."[5]

Several members of the political opposition pointed out the dangerous trajectory of the foreign debt. The government's reply to these criticisms was consistent: there was nothing to worry about because most of the debt was not a matter of state policies but of contracts between private Chilean financial groups and private foreign banks. Thus when the president of the Central Bank was asked if the government was concerned about how foreign credits were being invested, he replied in the negative: "This is a free economy. It is presumed that when individuals go into debt, they know what they are doing because they have to pay with their own capital."[6]

In a parallel action that culminated its anti-inflation policies, the government froze the price of the dollar in mid-1979. This measure was taken in the belief that with fixed exchange rates and free importation, internal prices could not rise more rapidly than global inflation. This orthodox monetary policy transformed the dollar into the cheapest merchandise in Chile. The country experienced a period of "easy money." Never before had the bourgeoisie and upper middle class been able to travel overseas and spend as freely, subsidized by a laughably cheap dollar. Within Chile, only the poorest classes were unable to purchase an enormous quantity and variety of imported products—automobiles, color televisions, perfume, liquor, toys, radios, and so on. The magnitude of this veritable carnival of import consumption has been well documented in the academic literature.

In the political realm, the civilian faction in the Cabinet reached its peak power in 1980, when it controlled the Ministry of Interior, all of the economic ministries, the Office of National Planning (Oficina de Planificación Nacional), and the Ministries of Labor, Mining (Minería) Agriculture, and Education. These "glory days" in the relationship between the civilian group and the military were enthusiastically described by the newspaper *El Mercurio* after the plebiscite on 11 September 1980:

> The politicians who permitted or created the state of affairs that led Chilean democracy to failure were defeated by the alliance between the military and the economists. This is the gist of the plebiscite of Thursday September 11. The military provided order, security, and confidence. The economists offered new ideas capable of raising the country from its knees and freeing energy to undertake the speedy march of development.... The military and the economists of this regime did the job left undone by the politicians who today desperately head the opposition.... That is the significance of the noteworthy alliance between the military and economists.[7]

This "holy alliance" of economists and the military also enjoyed the full support of the business world and the international banks in 1980.

The economists in the government and the heads of the large financial conglomerates had succeeded in establishing themselves as the keys to the Chilean economy's gaining access to international financial circles. Clearly, this role was the civilians' most significant contribution to the military regime, and it was doubly important because of the sorry state of Chile's relations with major Western governments since 1973.

In this atmosphere of political and economic euphoria, Pinochet recognized an opportunity to call a plebiscite to approve or disapprove a new constitution. The idea of creating a new constitution was almost as old as the regime itself. Forty-five days after the coup, the Military Junta had designated "a commission to study, elaborate, and propose a preliminary plan for a new national constitution."[8] The commission worked at a pace fittingly slow for a regime that had announced that it had goals but no timetable. After five years, the commission finished its assignment in October 1978 and turned over to Pinochet the fruit of its labor. Pinochet then sent the constitutional plan to the Council of State (Consejo de Estado) for study. The Council of State submitted its report to the Military Junta for consideration on 1 June 1980. On 10 August, Pinochet informed the nation that the project of writing a new constitution was finished and that he had scheduled a plebiscite for 11 September. Thus the constitutional commission took five years to draw up the new constitution, the Council of State took twenty-two months to analyze it and the Military Junta took forty days to approve it. But in just thirty days, the new constitution was to be discussed and voted on by the Chilean electorate.

According to the government, the results of the 1980 plebiscite favored the government's proposal. Some 67 percent of the voters approved the new constitution, while 30 percent voted against it. The opposition claimed, however, that the process was completely invalid because it lacked the minimum requirements of a fair plebiscite. It was asserted that a free election or plebiscite cannot take place in a country that is not free. During the brief thirty-day period between the announcement of the plebiscite and the voting, Chile was placed under a state of emergency, which meant that the government had the power to arrest or exile anyone. The opposition had absolutely no access to television and only limited access to newspapers. Within this context of extreme inequality of media and publicity resources, the country was subjected to a pervasive propaganda campaign carried out through all the means available to a dictatorship. The propaganda barrage combined the promise of a shining economic future with the threat of chaos and terror if the government's proposal was not approved.

In his speeches, General Pinochet pledged to create one million new jobs and build nine hundred thousand new homes during the transition period established by the Constitution of 1980. By the end of the 1980s, one in every seven Chileans would own an automobile, one in five would have a television, and one in seven would have a telephone. Minister of Labor José Piñera based these projections for 1985 on "serious studies": "In 1980 [there was] one vehicle for every 5.2 families, and in 1985 there could be one vehicle for every 2.5 families." The projected rate would have ranked Chile between Argentina and Spain in levels of automobile ownership. Similar progress was promised with regard to color television ownership. While 15 percent of the population had color television in 1980, 70 percent would have sets in 1985, matching the levels of Spain, Austria, and Italy.[9]

Meanwhile, ministers of state and leaders of large business associations were warning that rejecting Pinochet's proposed constitution would mean welcoming economic chaos in Chile. This campaign of intimidation peaked the day before the vote, when the daily *La Segunda*, then headed by Hermógenes Pérez de Arce (a vigorous supporter of the economic model), ran this headline across the entire front page: "List of Members of the Armed Forces Condemned to Death by Radio Moscow." At the top of the list was General Humberto Gordon (later the Army representative in the junta). Using extreme journalistic manipulation, the newspaper asked, "Will the communists carry out these sentences during the civic-military transition (proposed by Eduardo Frei in the name of the opposition as an alternative to Pinochet's constitution)?"[10] Thus the implication was made that voting "no" on the plebiscite would lead not only to economic chaos but to a blood bath as well.

Finally, during the period before the plebiscite, the military regime followed its standard practice of prohibiting all political parties and their activities. The very organization of the voting and vote-counting processes were also labeled invalid by the opposition. Voting took place without a list of voters. Chileans simply went to the polling place of their choice to cast ballots. To prevent double voting, each voter's right thumb was supposed to be marked with indelible ink, but instead, stamp pads and regular ink were used. Moreover, voting tables were supervised by government partisans. It has been amply documented that top business executives supervised the voting tables in poor suburban neighborhoods, while most of the supervisors and election judges at tables in the poorest areas of Santiago were upper-class women.

The form of vote counting, established in the special law written for the plebiscite, also left room for fraud at the local level. At each voting table, the votes were counted by the supervisor and election judges, who had been named by the mayor. Then the mayor, an appointee completely loyal to Pinochet, counted the votes, assisted only by his personally appointed municipal secretary.

By any objective standard of analysis, the 1980 plebiscite was a fraud that lacked the minimum qualifications of validity. But the government dismissed opposition complaints and protested any attempts to question "the honor and rectitude of those who controlled the process." When Andrés Zaldívar, the president of the Christian Democratic party, continued to make statements questioning the legitimacy of the plebiscite to the international press (the national press was strictly censored), the government exiled him for three years. By expelling the second-highest opposition leader (after Frei), the regime served notice nationally of its determination to punish any challenge to the legitimacy and validity of the 1980 plebiscite.

Adding to the deterioration in the morale and outlook of the Chilean opposition was the election of Ronald Reagan as President of the United States, which came three weeks after Zaldívar's expulsion and two months after the plebiscite. At that point, the opposition entered into a long period of silence. Nor were its assumptions about the new U.S. administration totally mistaken. During Reagan's first two and a half years in office at least, his administration showed itself to be favorably disposed toward the Pinochet regime. Thus although relations between the United States and the Chilean government had been rocky and distant during the Carter administration, in 1981 and 1982 they became sympathetic and cordial.

In February 1981, the Reagan administration lifted the prohibition on Export-Import Bank dealings with Chile and reinstated the invitation to the Chilean Navy to participate in Operation Unitas. In mid-1981 the Chilean minister of foreign relations (Relaciones Exteriores) made an official visit to the United States, which was reciprocated by a visit to Santiago by Jeane Kirkpatrick, the U.S. ambassador to the United Nations. Kirkpatrick was the first high-level U.S. official in some time to refuse to meet with the democratic opposition while in Chile. Chilean human-rights groups were also displeased by her announcement that the Reagan administration had decided to "close the Letelier case, based on the fact that all legal procedures have been exhausted... [and that] the relationship of Chilean government functionaries with the crime, if indeed it existed, was indirect."[11] It was therefore surprising when, forty-eight hours after the ambassador's visit, Pinochet exiled Jaime Castillo, the president of the Chilean Commission for Human Rights (Comisión Chilena de Derechos Humanos). This expulsion left Kirkpatrick, probably the most cordial U.S. government visitor the Pinochet regime has ever had, in an uncomfortable position.

As for Pinochet's never-ending drive to increase and personalize his power, the Constitution of 1980 was designed as a legal construct to extend his hold on power until 1997, that is, until the completion of twenty-five years of authoritarian rule.[12] Yet within the unified purpose of this document, three distinct phases can be discerned in the permanent and transitional articles. In each phase, power is structured differently, and the political role of the Armed Forces changes.

The first phase is the so-called transition period, which is regulated by the twenty-nine transitional articles of the constitution. This phase is scheduled to last eight years, from March 1981, when the constitution took effect, until the plebiscite and inauguration of the new President in 1989–1990.

During this transition period, the presidency is assigned *ad nominem* to General Pinochet, in terms that contradict an essential requisite of the rule of law: the requirement that "the prerogatives of office not be nominatively identified with the individuals who are ruling."[13] In defiance of that criterion, Transitional Article 14 of the Constitution of 1980 provides that from 1981 to 1989, "the current President, Army General Señor Augusto Pinochet Ugarte, will continue as President of the Republic."

During this period, the junta will continue to exist, "made up of the Commanders in Chief of the Army, the Navy, and the Air Force, and the Director General of the National Police." It is clear nevertheless that the transitional articles of the Constitution of 1980 comprise a further step in transforming the Military Junta into a subordinate political body.

Transitional Article 14 formally reduces the status of the Military Junta by stipulating that General Pinochet "will not be a member of the Governing Junta and will designate in his place, as titular member of the junta, the General of the Army who follows him in seniority." The contrast seems almost too obvious between the tenuous position of the junta members and the tailor-made security of General Pinochet's presidency.

In fact, since this disposition took effect, the post of Army representative to the Military Junta has certainly been precarious. To begin with, it has always been filled by a lieutenant general, a rank assigned to general officers who have reached retirement age and who remain in the Army only by special dispensation from General Pinochet. Moreover, the position has been characterized by a high rate of turnover: the first appointee, Raúl Benavides, lasted four and a half years; the second, Julio Canessa, scarcely one year; and the third, Humberto Gordon, has held the post only since January 1987.

The transitional articles of the constitution also effectively limit the Military Junta to legislative functions and the exercise of constituent authority. As a legislative body, the junta is authorized to adopt measures only by unanimous agreement. This rule means that the Military Junta cannot exercise any control over the executive branch without the gracious permission of the Chief of State and his replacement on the junta. On the other side of this extremely asymmetrical power structure, no legislation can be passed without General Pinochet's approval. Although it could be argued that all members of the Military Junta, not just General Pinochet, retain veto power over the decision-making process, this power is a purely negative exercise that would end up destroying the very entity of which it is a part.

All these examples illustrate the degree to which the Military Junta has been subordinated to the Chief of State through constitutional provisions. In the exercise of constituent authority, the junta must again act unanimously, and its decisions on constitutional reforms are subject to ratification by plebiscite.

During this extended "transition period" (eight years), civilians are entirely excluded from the power structure. The election of a Congress is not projected until 1989. Nor is any kind of local participation allowed, it remaining the President's prerogative "to freely designate and remove mayors throughout the entire country."[14] Moreover, Transitional Disposition 24 effectively deprives the civilian population of basic constitutional rights throughout the transition period. This constitutional article formalizes the President's power—unrestrained by judicial process—to arrest, exile or send into internal exile any citizen, and to bar any citizen from entering the country. The constitution specifies that such means "will not be subject to any recourse except reconsideration by the authority that imposed them." The President's authority to restrict the right of assembly and the freedom to found, publish, or circulate new publications is also unchecked.

This second phase is to last through 11 March 1989, a period obviously characterized by extreme concentration of power in the hands of General Pinochet. Beyond the already-noted political functions of the four commanders in chief, the military has no real role in determining government policy in Chile.

CHAPTER 6

The End of the "Miracle"

The euphoria of the 1980 plebiscite had not ebbed when the "economic miracle" burst like a balloon. The "miracle" had been, in certain ways, a speculative bubble. On the positive side, inflation had been reduced from rates exceeding 300 percent in 1974 and 1975 to 30 percent in 1980. The fiscal situation had also improved in that the large deficit had been reduced to almost nothing. In terms of production, one significant change had been achieved with the development of exports other than copper. Other aspects of the economy, however, were performing poorly. The economic growth rate between 1974 and 1980 lagged far behind those of democratic regimes. In actuality, growth had been confused with economic recovery. Production increases through 1978 recovered only the 13 percent decline in the gross domestic product of 1975. As has been observed by one economic analyst, "it was obviously incorrect to project long-term growth rates resulting from this recovery, especially when taking into account the low volume of investments in those years.... During all the years of the so-called miracle, the investment rate—measured in comparable terms—remained significantly below levels of the 1960s."[1] Moreover, the low growth recorded in those years was concentrated in the service sector, particularly in financial services, and not in productive sectors such as industry, agriculture, and mining.

What also became evident was the high social cost of the "miracle." The unemployment rate had risen 300 percent above the historic mean, and wages never recovered the levels reached in the late 1970s. Per capita spending on housing, education, and health also diminished in comparison with the amounts spent by the Frei and Allende governments.

The implosion of the "Chilean economic miracle" was as thunderous as the image of its success had been illusory. Governmental authorities, businessmen, banks, and the mass media associated with the right or the regime all denied the existence of a threatening economic situation, refusing to recognize that the economy had entered a severe crisis. In late 1981, official sources were still maintaining that the country would have a 3 percent annual growth rate in 1982. "It's not that we will not grow," said one high-level economic authority, "but that we will grow less."

At this juncture, the international banking system must at least be mentioned. The enormous foreign debt accumulated by Chile has typically been viewed in the international financial community as a result of irresponsibility and bad management by Chileans. It has been contended that the Chilean government did not adequately oversee use of the monies and that the financial conglomerates went into debt beyond all reason and failed to channel resources into investment. While the foregoing view is absolutely true, it is also incomplete because it fails to take into account the other party responsible for this monumental failure—the international private banking system.

Curiously, 1981 was not only the year in which the "economic miracle" burst but also the year when the greatest abundance of credits was extended by the international banks to private Chilean businesses. More than four billion dollars were loaned without government guarantee, an amount equaling 40 percent of all loans of this type obtained between 1974 and 1981.[2] The role played by the international banks has been pointed out by opposition economists such as Aníbal Pinto,[3] but also by Arnold Harberger, the University of Chicago professor named by the Chilean press as the "spiritual father" of the "Chicago Boys": "The international banking community has made Chile its favorite for several years. Bankers came from all over the world to try to offer new credits to Chile.... Part of the blame also falls on the international bankers, whose enthusiasm seems to have exceeded their prudence in the Chilean case.... These foreign bankers simply did not do their job well; they did not look beneath the façade to discover the real nature of the portfolios of the Chilean banks."

The enthusiasm of the international private banks was actually stimulated by such organizations as the World Bank and the International Monetary Fund. In September 1981, when the crisis had become evident to everyone, the World Bank was still describing Chilean economic prospects in these terms. "[G]ood growth prospects and continued sound financial management should keep Chile as one of the most creditworthy of the developing countries during the 1980s."[5]

In late 1981, Chile's financial crisis became even more acute. The gross national product fell 15 percent and unemployment exceeded 25 percent of the work force. In the early days of November 1981, the government decreed a state takeover of four banks (Banco Español, Banco de Talca, Banco de Fomento de Valparaíso, and Banco de Linares) and of four other financial institutions (Compañía General Financiera, Financiera de Capitales, Finansur, and Financiera Cash). Notwithstanding the seriousness of these decisions, the private sector and the press supporting the economic model characterized the measure as "inevitable": "The takeovers have succeeded in providing the public with security and have permitted market operations to continue normally." The vice-president of the Central Bank, Hernán Felipe Errázuriz, stated: "The foreign banks have reacted positively to the improvements that have been undertaken in the banking system."[6]

Meanwhile, bank balances for 1981 (published in 1982) exhibited worrisome signs. Profits had diminished greatly and some banks showed losses. Defaulted loans climbed to 2.3 percent of total loans, an extremely large percentage considering that in the United States, a level of 0.4 percent is judged to represent a sharp deterioration.[7]

The crisis continued to worsen, forcing the state to take over two more banks (Banco Austral and Banco de Fomento de Bío-Bío) in 1982. In early July, the government made a desperate attempt to stem the crisis by announcing its decision to buy the banking system's defaulted and high-risk loans. This measure, which stirred public opinion deeply, was again presented as "inevitable" in order to save the system from a collapse that would have dragged the entire economy down.

But the crisis seemed to be unstoppable. On 31 October, the defaulted loans of the financial system, including those already bought by the Central Bank, totaled 10 percent of all loans, excluding those held by the Banco del Estado. On 13 January 1982, the situation reached its climax when the government liquidated three financial institutions (Financiera CIGA, Banco Hipotecario de Chile, and Banco Unido de Fomento) and appointed the directors of five other banks (Banco de Chile, Banco de Santiago, Banco de Concepción, Banco Internacional, and Banco Colocadora Nacional de Valores). The latter measure was extremely serious because the affected banks were major institutions: the Banco de Chile, the Banco de Santiago, and the Banco de Concepción ranked as the first-, second- and fifth-most-important commercial banking institutions in the country.

Above all, this measure debilitated the two most powerful financial conglomerates of the era: the Cruzat-Larraín group, owned by Manuel Cruzat and Fernando Larraín, and the Vial group, headed by Javier Vial. The backbone of the first group had been the Santiago and Colocadora banks; the second group had relied on the Banco de Chile and the Banco Hipotecario de Chile. These conglomerates had originally been formed as a direct result of the policies of the "Chicago Boys." The two conglomerates controlled the largest Chilean private enterprises and were broadly diversified, extending from the banks to the mass media to important mining, agricultural, industrial, and construction firms. These two groups were also the largest debtors in the Chilean banking system and the largest private debtors to foreign banks.

The relations of these conglomerates with the political system, particularly with the government's economic team, were so close that they violated minimal standards on conflict of interest. Presidents and advisors of Cruzat-Larraín banks and businesses accepted positions in the most important economic ministries, while government ministers became presidents of banks and group-owned businesses when they left their government posts. Ministers Jorge Cauas, Pablo Barahona, José Piñera, and Alfonso Márquez de la Plata are only a few of those involved in these links. Long after leaving the Ministry of the Economy, Sergio de Castro assumed a high position in the Edwards group, which owned *El Mercurio*, the largest Chilean newspaper.

Thus in only fifteen months, governmental authorities had taken over or liquidated thirteen banks and five other financial institutions, ordered the merger of others to prevent their collapse, and provided enormous sums of money to shore up the private financial system. In mid 1983, only seven of the nineteen Chilean commercial banks in Chile had not been taken over or liquidated, and only eight of twenty-two investment banks (*bancos de fomento*) and other financial intermediaries (*financieras*) had escaped liquidation or state control. By the end of 1983, the defaults, including those sold to the Central Bank, totaled 17 percent of all loans, while high-risk loans made up another 15 percent of that sum. The net losses of the banks equaled 242 percent of their capital and reserves.[8]

Naturally, the banks' difficulties were only one dimension of the economic disaster. The situation in industry was equally or more dramatic. The only difference was that their problems—manifested as bankruptcies, suspended loan payments, and massive layoffs—lacked the spectacular newsworthiness of the bank crises. Jorge Fontaine, president of the Confederation of Production and Commerce (Confederación de la Producción y del Comercio) likened the productive firms to dying elephants whose bones would be left on the shore.

The bank takeovers and liquidations meant not only that those institutions passed into the hands of the state but that many of the enormous assets of the large financial groups did so as well. These gains were augmented by the sale of many other firms whose owners were unable to meet their financial responsibilities and had to forfeit their businesses in payment to the banking system, now overwhelmingly under state control. Thus Chile's exceedingly neoliberal economic policy suddenly ended with state involvement in the economy as complete as it was involuntary. By early 1983 the experiment of the "Chicago Boys" appeared to the country as a striking example of a policy that had defeated itself.

Moreover, an economic crisis this deep was incubating a major social and political crisis. During the second quarter of 1983, the unemployment rate (which included those receiving

unemployment subsidies) rose to 34 percent. This figure could well translate into unemployment rates above 50 percent in many poor neighborhoods. Unemployment among the youth in those areas was even higher, 60 percent or more. These estimatesss were corroborated by priests and social leaders living in the neighborhoods. Furthermore, social spending per capita decreased 20 percent between 1974 and 1982, while public investment in the social sector decreased by 80 percent.[9]

The resulting social picture could hardly have been more dramatic or explosive: drastic increases in unemployment, reduction of purchasing power of those who still had jobs, reduction of the real value of pensions and family subsidies, and extreme deterioration in basic social services. Yet these figures say nothing about the effects of poverty on families and the social fabric. Empirical studies have repeatedly confirmed high correlations between drug addiction, child prostitution, and similar social ills, on one hand, and the poverty and desperation associated with lack of work and income, on the other.[10]

The effects of the crisis and the government's ill-conceived economic policies to combat it led to a situation that was aptly described to me by a high-level banker: "The Central Bank took a hard line with us; we passed along the effects to our debtors, who are individuals or businesses that create demand and employment; our debtors reduced their demand, dismissed some of their workers, and lowered the wages of the others. By means of this 'conveyor belt,' the pressure accumulated mainly in poor neighborhoods, where you find the overwhelming concentration of suffering created by this social volcano on which we now live."

Throughout this period, the situation regarding human rights remained bleak. In 1981 and 1982, according to records of the Vicariate of Solidarity, 125 torture victims testified before the Tribunals of Justice (Tribunales de Justicia). The true number of victims must be higher, given that most victims of such abuses choose not to report the crimes, fearing reprisals or being unwilling to relive the inhuman and degrading treatment to which they were subjected.

In this atmosphere of deep economic and social crisis and in the absence of political rights, Chile was rocked by a series of events that began on 11 May 1983. The Copper Workers Union (Confederación de Trabajadores del Cobre) under the leadership of Rodolfo Seguel, called a general strike against the dictatorship. But it quickly became obvious that such a strike was absolutely impossible, given the repressive force of the regime, the weakness of the trade unions, and the hundreds of thousands of unemployed (the reserve army of the unemployed that Karl Marx had described a century before) available to take the jobs of those who would be dismissed for having participated in a strike. Given these circumstances, the call for a general strike was replaced by an ambiguous call for "a national day of protest."

The outcome surprised everyone. The evening of 11 May 1983, the capital city of Santiago, especially middle-class and upper-middle-class neighborhoods, reverberated with the deafening noise of Chileans beating on pots and pans and honking car horns to express their profound dissatisfaction with the military regime.

CHAPTER 7

The Protests:
Rise and Fall of
the Popular Struggle
(1983–1986)

The periodic protests that began in 1983 became the first mass demonstrations against the dictatorship. The first few protests consisted of nonviolent activities, such as banging on pots and pans at a specified hour, honking car horns, boycotting all stores and markets, and keeping children home from school. Political and social leaders held unauthorized meetings in public plazas as symbolic acts of dissent, and industrial workers staged work slowdowns. Subsequent protests included more confrontational activities, such as tire bonfires, sit-ins, and barricades placed to disrupt traffic.[1]

When these protests attracted international attention, many groups inside and outside Chile began to hope that the unrest would bring down the dictatorship. Once it became evident that Pinochet was not going to fall, however, the protests lost momentum and their impact on Chilean society declined. The protest of 2–3 July 1986 was probably the last significant demonstration against the regime. By that time, the conflict that had torn Chile apart for three years had cost at least one hundred lives on protest days alone. Opposition sources claim that the death toll was substantially higher.

The first protest occurred on 11 May 1983. It enjoyed strong support among the middle and upper middle classes and consisted mainly of noisemaking with pots and pans and car horns. But although the demonstrators' purpose was nonviolent protest, the government's repressive response resulted in two deaths, fifty injuries, and three hundred arrests.

The second protest took place on 14 June 1983, with the middle and upper-middle classes again participating in large numbers. Also taking part were many residents of the poor neighborhoods that ring Santiago. The most important outcome of the June protest was the call by the trade unions for an indefinite national strike in response to the arrests of Rodolfo Seguel and other leaders of the Copper Workers Union. The strike, however, ended in complete failure.

The third protest occurred on 12 July. A few days before, several leaders of the Christian Democratic party had been arrested, among them Gabriel Valdés and Jorge Lavanderos. These arrests became the focus of protest activities during July. The fourth protest, on 11 August, coincided with the appointment of Sergio Onofre Jarpa as minister of interior. The first civilian to be named to this post in Pinochet's cabinet, Jarpa was assigned responsibility for initiating a "dialogue" with the democratic opposition.

The government reacted brutally to the July and August demonstrations. An 8:00 p.m. curfew was declared for 12 July and 6:00 p.m. curfew for 11 August. During the August protest, Pinochet addressed the nation, informing Chileans that he had assigned eighteen thousand soldiers to occupy Santiago the night of 11 August "with instructions to be tough." The force of the government repression was massive. Yet official figures for the third protest listed only two deaths. The fourth protest met with an even more violent response. Official figures claimed twenty nine dead and one hundred wounded, while responsible opposition organizations reported that more than eighty had died.

The most salient aspect of the third and fourth protests was the decline in support among certain sectors of society. Starting with the fourth protest, middle and upper-middle class support dwindled as the protest movement lost significance for the members of those social strata. The protests were rapidly becoming an expression of predominantly lower-class discontent, with their greatest support from young Chileans in poor neighborhoods.

The fifth protest, called for 8 September, proved to be the last to be identified by number. Up through the fifth, each protest evidenced characteristics and events that distinguished it from the others. After the fifth, however, no subsequent protest would compare in strength and intensity with the first five.

It seems reasonable to end these detailed descriptions with the fifth protest because by September 1983, the movement had become torn apart by contradictions that were to end its political effectiveness. The first contradiction was the myth of the national strike, which had emerged after the second protest. The arrests of the leaders of Copper Workers' Union provoked a hastily called strike, with the copper miners being the main participants. The government immediately fired eighteen hundred strikers, which completely destroyed the strike. Moreover, the struggle to reinstate the fired workers absorbed the energies of trade union leaders for the next two years and more.

This failed strike represented the trade unions' first and last attempt to take a leading role in the protests. The strike also became a negative example to other unions of what could happen if they struck. Thereafter, the large unions limited themselves to simply participating in the protests; no union tried again to bring national activity to a standstill, nor was there any call for a new strike immediately after the failed work stoppage in June 1983. But although a national strike had been shown to be a practical impossibility, the idea of such a strike retained enormous power—to the point that belief in it became for some an emotional necessity rather than a rational conviction.

The idea resurfaced in March 1984 as the result of a series of successful protest activities that kindled false hopes for an effective strike. It was as if the misleading impression that a national strike could be successful had been deliberately created. Without a work stoppage being called, the March protest had all the effects of a strike. Fear of harsh repression, added to the government's miscalculation in decreeing an 8:30 p.m. curfew, caused activity in Santiago to cease by early afternoon. Stores began to close after midday, and public transportation was scarce after 3:00 p.m. Employees in offices and factories were dismissed early out of fear that they would be stranded in an empty city without transportation.

At that point, Chile's most radical sectors began to envision a national strike as an imminent possibility. Nevertheless, none of the protests in the next six months succeeded. Yet during the September 1984 protest, the false prospect of a national strike re-emerged. On 4 September, activity in the capital city ground to a halt by early afternoon. But activity returned to normal on the second day of the protest, and hopes for a national strike waned.

Prompted by events in September the National Workers' Command (Comando Nacional de Trabajadores) called a national strike for 30 October, the second of two scheduled days of protest. This time the results were inconclusive. The initiators and organizers, including the Communist party and the radical left, declared the strike a success. But the rest of the opposition found it difficult to judge how much of the effect was due to the trade union strike, which they considered relatively small, and how much was due to the same conditions that had existed in March and September. A week later, on 6 November, the government reimposed a state of siege, and thoughts of a strike, as well as any attempts at social mobilization or protest, were deferred until the following year.

From mid-1985 through July 1986, the desire for a general strike was kept alive in many opposition circles. It became a catchword that few (if any) dared challenge, although any analysis of the workers' movement and the overall situation in Chile would have led to the conclusion that such a tactic was futile. The opposition probably came closest to achieving a national strike on 2–3 July 1986. Even this strike, however, was far from successful. Manuel Antonio Garretón has observed that this mobilization showed "the predominance of middle sectors and the scant presence of the working class, which had the lowest level of participation in the strike." The impact of the strike on the regime was due "fundamentally to national and international reaction to the repression, including the military forces' burning of two young people, one of whom died."[2]

But even then, a national strike proved to be infeasible. The main reason that a national strike could not succeed was a reality as old as the workers' movement—what Karl Marx termed the "reserve army of the unemployed." The closer a society comes to full employment, the more possible a workers' strike becomes; conversely, when unemployment is high, a strike becomes more difficult. To "discipline" the working world in Chile, the Pinochet regime has wielded a far more effective tool than the secret police—endemic unemployment and hundreds of thousands of underemployed workers who want stable, well-paying jobs. These unemployed workers are the "reserve army" that Pinochet maintains as a deterrent to anyone who might want to initiate a strike.

The problem facing the labor leadership was obvious: how to call a general strike when the workers were facing not only the threat of police repression but unemployment and the consequent inability to feed their families. Moreover, the union movement had been greatly weakened during the dictatorship. The movement had lost affiliates and resources and was operating in a brutally hostile environment. To undertake its greatest effort in its hour of greatest weakness was, to say the least, naive.

Thus the possibility of a successful strike against the Pinochet regime was one of the great myths of the protests and an element that contributed to their failure. But banking on a national labor strike—or a general political strike—was not the opposition's only error. Another was overestimating the political potency of those living in the *poblaciones* (working-class neighborhoods).

After the second protest (on 14 June 1983), the trade unions ceased to be a significant force in the protest movement. Middle-class participation began to decline during the fourth and fifth protests (in August and September 1983), and the protests increasingly became a movement of the poor. But what was the political power of demonstrators who were almost entirely the unemployed, students, and youth from the *poblaciones*? Lacking the support of either unions or the middle sectors, popular protest against a brutal dictatorship was reduced to militant action. The history of social struggles has shown that such a movement could not overcome a dictatorship. Thus the opposition's conception of the potential of the *población* movement was more romantic than real.

But what was the *población* movement? What was the make-up of the social group that became the central protagonist in the protests? It was not the proletariat, which, in the classic sense, accounted for less than one-sixth of those living in the *poblaciones*. According to a survey of *población* dwellers in Santiago conducted by SUR in 1985, 18 percent of the heads of households were unemployed. Of those who had jobs, only 17 percent worked in industry and construction, while 18 percent worked for a paltry monthly stipend in government occupational subsidy programs like PEM (Programa de Empleo Mínimo) and POJH (Programa de Ocupación para Jefes de Hogar). The other 65 percent consisted of marginal vendors (14 percent), artisans and self-employed workers (11 percent), salaried transport workers (8 percent), and domestic workers (6 percent), or they held assorted other jobs.[3]

Furthermore, the *población* movement, like the trade unions, had fallen victim to the military regime's policy of destroying popular organizations. As a result, during the protest years, the *poblaciones* were comprised of a mass of unorganized individuals and a few isolated, weak, and unfinanced organizations of several thousand residents. Most of these organizations were oriented not toward politics but toward more basic objectives such as establishing soup kitchens, self-help groups, and shopping cooperatives.

Such a situation, in which the inherent weakness of the sector was aggravated by its extreme heterogeneity, created the conditions that gave rise to one of the most ineffective forms of political violence. Robert Dowse and John Hughes have defined this "turmoil" as "relatively spontaneous and unorganized violence with quite widespread popular support and participation which includes strikes, riots and rebellions. This form of violence is associated with the relatively intense deprivations among the mass of people or a particular mass of people who tend to be rather badly organized, lacking highly articulated political parties, lacking access to state bureaucracies and who are generally badly integrated into the society."[4]

The turmoil of the protests increased, exacerbated by misery and the lack of political outlets in the *poblaciones*. Senseless violence against lives and property, committed by the unemployed in their own neighborhoods, became an expression of frustration over years of joblessness. The government's brutally repressive action only intensified this kind of violence. In this explosive situation, the Communist party articulated a policy of complete support and validation of the "spontaneousness" of such protest and its accompanying violence. In the Communists' view, as expressed in documents and declarations by party leaders, no action by the masses should be forbidden in the struggle against Pinochet. No action should be condemned. Any kind of behavior was acceptable, from vandalism and pillage to unarmed men throwing rocks at security forces.[5]

Clearly, these activities by groups of unarmed youths, who were always vulnerable to infiltration by lumpen proletariat and by the police, could not even dent the dictatorship. Moreover, the struggles took place on the periphery of Santiago, outside the industrial areas and far from the political and financial center. What the Communist party and the extreme left refused to understand was that such violence was not only completely ineffective in the struggle against the government, it was also the most effective way to destroy the protest movement. The government's propaganda machine cleverly portrayed the violence as simple vandalism and used this notion to isolate the *poblaciones* further. The violent dissent, which had become possible as Chileans' fear of the state decreased, generated what has been aptly described as a process of fear of the state being replaced by fear of society—of a society's own self-destructive tendencies as manifested in the protests.[6]

This fear was not limited to the upper and middle classes but also extended to the *poblaciones*, the world of the workers, the unemployed, and the marginalized. The imposition of a state of siege in November 1984 actually met with stronger approval among the popular sectors than among the middle and upper strata. Although the majority of *población* residents supported the opposition, they were weary and afraid of the violence that had been unleashed in their neighborhoods on protest days by protestors and government agents (some in uniform and others secretly affiliated).[7]

In March 1984, the protests began to evolve and be channeled by the extremists (the "ultras") into another unusual tactic. Because the workers had failed to effect a national strike, the new plan was to use the threat of violence to compel merchants and urban transport owners to suspend activities. The idea was that closing businesses and interrupting bus service would provoke the general strike that the unions had been unable to achieve. A more simplistic view of the dynamics of a national strike would be hard to find.

Not surprisingly, this national strike never took place. At times when success seemed near, informed observers were drawn to an ironic conclusion: those who were neither interested in nor committed to a general strike nontheless participated, while those who would have liked to participate were unable to do so. That is to say, stores were closed and buses did not run, but no important trade union struck or even produced significant levels of absenteeism.

The nature of human-rights violations changed throughout the course of the protests. While reports of torture and excessive force continued, a new kind of repression was directed at entire neighborhoods. Between 1976 and 1982, the annual number of arrests recorded by the Catholic Vicariate of Solidarity seldom surpassed fifteen hundred. In 1976, 1977, and 1981 fewer than one thousand arrests were made annually. But the number of arrests rose from 1213 in 1982, to 4537 in 1983, 5291 in 1984, 5314 in 1985, and 7019 in 1986. The Vicariate explained that this sevenfold increase in arrests was intended to create "a general atmosphere of fear in the *poblaciones* and to discourage the eventual recurrence of collective dissidence or protest." Nine-tenths of those arrested in 1984 "were freed after hours or days of arbitrary deprivation of liberty, with no charges filed against them."[8]

The government also arrested protest leaders, especially in the *poblaciones*, in response to opposition activities. The detainees were eventually sent to internal exile in isolated and unhospitable regions of Chile. In 1982, the year before the protests began, internal exiles totaled 60; in 1983 this figure rose to 127, and in 1984 to 727.[9]

But perhaps the most disturbing manifestation of the new repression were the "neighborhood sweeps." Carried out in poor areas by joint forces of the Army, the National Police, and the secret police, these operations were reminiscent of the actions of foreign armies of occupation or the roundups carried out by French paratroopers in Muslim areas during the Algerian war of 1954–1962. In the middle of the night during the curfew, heavily armed troops with numerous vehicles and armored personnel carriers would encircle a *población*. Awakening the residents with loudspeakers, secret police, intelligence personnel, and uniformed police would enter the area and search each home. All men over age fifteen were detained in a stadium or plaza for the rest of the day. At dusk, most of the detainees were freed, but activists associated with the protests and those wanted for common crimes were held for several days or sent into internal exile. Thus these sweep-and-search operations were acts of state terrorism used by the regime to intimidate the *poblaciones* and deactivate the protests.

If the sole objective of the protests is viewed as overthrowing Pinochet, then the protest movement failed. But this blanket statement masks a more complex outcome. The Chilean opposition did secure significant liberties as a result of the pressure exerted by the protests, and in this sense, the movement did not fail.

Following the second protest in June 1983, the government ended book censorship, which had been one of the dictatorship's most abhorrent measures against freedom of expression. The protests also created breathing room for news and opinion magazines. It should be recalled that the Constitution of 1980 had instituted strict government control of the media, and the "establishment, publication, or circulation of new publications" (that is, newspapers and magazines) had to be authorized by the minister of interior, who had systematically denied permission. But under the pressure of the protests, the government authorized publication of the social democratic weekly *Cauce* in November 1983. Four months later, a group headed by Jorge Lavanderos (one of the most active instigators of the protest movement) acquired *Fortín Mapocho*, an inconsequential magazine that had circulated sporadically among the small merchants in Santiago's municipal market. Lavanderos transformed the magazine first into a national newsweekly and then, in early 1987, into a daily. Besieged by the ongoing social unrest, the dictatorship had to accept Lavanderos's end run around the legal requirement of government authorization.

Moreover, two magazines that had been quiescent under the rigid censorship existing before May 1983 rapidly became national magazines with a decided opposition tone: *Apsi* was associated with revisionist socialism, and *Análisis*, also committed to the left, with an undercurrent of Communist party influence.

These magazines were subjected to various threats, legal actions, and suspensions. The most serious was the seven-month suspension of *Cauce*, *Apsi*, *Análisis*, and *Fortín Mapocho* beginning in October 1984. At the same time, prior censorship was decreed for *Hoy*, the most influential weekly in the country.

The situation of the broadcast media can be illustrated by what happened to the opposition radio stations. Under the dictatorship, the importance and influence of television news programming had diminished, but the news programming of two radio stations acquired unprecedented listenership. The two influential stations were Radio Chilena, owned by the Santiago Archdiocese, and Radio Cooperativa, owned by a group of Christian Democrats. Surveys in 1983 showed that Radio Cooperativa's news programs enjoyed greater credibility than any other communication outlet in Chile. In June 1983, the news programs of both Radio Cooperativa and Radio Chilena were temporarily suspended by the military authorities. The same thing happened in March 1984 for ten days, and again on 4 September and 24 October 1984. On 29 October, these stations were ordered to transmit official news only, a restriction that lasted two weeks.

The protests also wrought significant changes in other realms of society. Until 1983 Pinochet controlled the selection of the directors of organizations of students, attorneys, doctors, engineers, architects, and other professionals. But social pressure destroyed the "labor peace," and these social sectors won the right to elect their leaders beginning in

1984 and 1985. As a result of this change, the opposition gained overwhelming majorities in student and professional organizations.

Yet it must be remembered that none of the opposition's gains were achieved without dozens of innocent deaths, thousands of arrests, and serious abuses of fundamental rights. The government conceded freedoms against its will, while constantly trying to regain its previous level of control. But despite the military regime's relentless countermeasures, by the time the protests had stopped, freedom of the press as well as other civil liberties had been restored in Chile to a degree that would have seemed inconceivable in late 1982.

CHAPTER 8

The Conflict between the Moderate Opposition and the Armed Opposition (1983–1987)

The effects of the protests went beyond greater freedom of the press and the opposition's recovery of control over civilian organizations. The social agitation that began in May 1983 also significantly changed Chile's relationship with the United States. As the protests gained momentum, the sympathy shown toward Chile during the first years of the Reagan administration gave way to growing disapproval. This trend became especially apparent after a state of siege was decreed in Chile in November 1984.

Two U.S. government appointments in particular affected the Pinochet regime adversely. The first was the naming in May 1985 of Elliott Abrams as Assistant Secretary of State for Inter-American Affairs. Abrams succeeded Langhorne Motley, a Pinochet sympathizer. In his previous post as U.S. Secretary of State for Human Rights and Humanitarian Affairs, Abrams had demonstrated concern over issues significant to the Chilean opposition. The second important change occurred in August 1985, when the U.S. ambassador to Chile, James Theberge, was replaced. Appointed in 1982, he had embodied the Reagan administration's closest ties with Pinochet, and his conservative bias had virtually cut him off from the Chilean opposition. Theberge was succeeded by Henry Barnes, a career diplomat who previously had served as ambassador to India. Barnes's appointment was interpreted in Chile as a major setback for the military regime.

Another effect of the protests was to open unprecedented space for political party activism within Chile. In reality, the Christian Democratic party had never stopped being active, despite the laws dissolving and proscribing political parties. The Communist party had resumed its activities in the late 1970s and the Socialists re-emerged in the same period although they split in 1980 into a Marxist-Leninist faction and a revisionist Marxist faction. The first group favored an alliance with the Communists, while the second inclined toward the European Social Democrats internationally and collaboration with the Christian Democrats domestically.

The Christian Democratic party had continued to be more active than the Socialist and Communist parties during the harshest years of the dictatorship partly because the Christian Democrats ran less risk of violent repression. The greatest personal risk for Christian Democrats was exile, while for Communists, it was death. When the protests began, three former presidents of the Chilean Christian Democratic party were in exile: Jaime Castillo, Renán Fuentealba, and Andrés Zaldívar. In contrast, ten Communist party leaders had been added to the lists of the "arrested and disappeared" following the secret police's ambush of the offices of the Central Committee of the Communist party in 1976.

Meanwhile, the parties of the right had kept themselves in a cocoon. Except for a small group of respectable but uninfluential conservatives, the traditional sectors had neither organized themselves nor felt the need to denounce government policies. They lived in a separate world, not noticing—or more precisely, trying not to notice—the exilings, human-rights violations, and mistakes and injustices of the government's economic policy.

In July 1983, after the third protest, the activism of the moderate opposition parties crystallized into the Democratic Alliance (Alianza Democrática, or AD), a coalition of six groups: from the right, the Republican party; from the center, the Radical, Social Democratic, and Christian Democratic parties; and from the left, the Socialist party and the small Popular Socialist Union (Unión Socialista Popular). The Communist party was excluded from the alliance on the grounds that it advocated the use of violence.

On 5 August 1983, the democratic opposition celebrated its reunification with a well-attended luncheon at a Santiago club. The founding document of the Democratic Alliance stated, "As individuals with differing political, philosophical, and religious positions, we unite in agreeing to respect and promote certain ethical principles and values that democracy upholds, without which a free, prosperous, just, and fraternal society is not possible."[1] For the first time in two decades, those who in the past had supported the conservative government of Jorge Alessandri (1958–1964), the reformist government of Eduardo Frei (1964–1970), and the revolutionary government of Salvador Allende (1970–1973) came together in political accord.

A week after the creation of the Democratic Alliance, Pinochet named Sergio Onofre Jarpa, a right-wing civilian, as minister of interior. With the Archbishop of Santiago, Juan Francisco Fresno, acting as mediator, Jarpa opened a dialogue with the Democratic Alliance. Days after the dialogue began, the Communists put together the Popular Democratic Movement (Movimiento Democrático Popular) in response to what they described as the faltering attitude of the Democratic Alliance. Led by the Communist party, the Popular Democratic Movement coalition included the wing of the Socialist party headed by Clodomiro Almeyda and the MIR, an extreme leftist group with a long history of armed struggle.

Thus as a consequence of the dialogue, the opposition split into two coalitions. But the high political cost of the break between the moderate and the radicalized left could not be justified by success—the dialogue collapsed in early October, scarcely six weeks after it began. The breakdown was so irreparable that negotiations have never resumed.

The discussions began on 25 August 1983 and moved slowly toward a basis for agreement. Francisco Bulnes, a right-wing leader and former senator who had served for a time as Pinochet's ambassador to Peru, accompanied Minister of Interior Jarpa to the negotiations. Bulnes later commented, "I attended the last meeting of the dialogue...and suggested in general terms my own formula.... [M]y proposition was quite well received at first, with the parties agreeing to study it and meet soon to take it up; but a few days later, in an informal talk in the countryside, the President declared that the participants could engage in as much dialogue as they liked, but he would make no concessions of any kind. Faced with this declaration, the Democratic Alliance cut off the dialogue because there was no reason to continue if one of the parties was determined beforehand to make no concessions."[2] Pinochet declared, "Dialogue can be developed and consensus sought, but the path has been chosen, and we, the Armed Forces, are sworn to follow that path and will proceed at any cost."[3]

After the dialogue foundered, Chile became torn apart by the contradictory political strategies of the democratic opposition, the opposition dominated by the Communist party, and General Pinochet. These new groupings divided the protest movement and the opposition as a whole into a controversy over the methods of political struggle—a conflict that has thus far remained insurmountable. The Democratic Alliance and the Popular Democratic Movement attempted to implement protest strategies that were not only different but antagonistic.

The Democratic Alliance viewed the protests as the social pressure that should bring the government to negotiations. Thus social mobilization and negotiation were not considered antithetical but rather two tactical steps of a single strategy. In contrast, the Popular Democratic Movement viewed the protests as the first step in a policy of mass insurrection that rejected both dialogue and negotiation with the government. The protests were to be part of a strategy that included a civilian organization (the Communist party and the Popular Democratic Movement), an armed branch (the FPMR or Frente Popular Manuel Rodríguez), and a paramilitary structure (the "Rodriguista Militias").

The protests resumed in March 1984, but this time, with a new component: increasing violence that was being fomented by armed groups. During the first protest of 1984, the FPMR (the armed branch of the Communist party) emerged publicly. Subsequent demonstrations included subway bombings, railway and bus sabotage, and attacks on and assassinations of National Police (Carabineros). Armed groups also dynamited high-voltage electrical towers, causing power failures in large areas of the country.

In November 1984, this insurrectional strategy was verbalized in a manifesto: "The FPMR has concluded that the only way to efficiently confront and bring down this regime is by making use of all forms of combat, including armed struggle. For precisely this reason, our Front has been constituted—to lead the people militarily in their struggle toward the final victory."[4] The FPMR maintained that the protests demonstrated a coalescence of political and social forces that favored the people.

What, then, was lacking to achieve victory? "It is necessary" the FPMR stated, "for the people to confront the task of building their military forces." This undertaking required "the unity of the various armed detachments of the people in order to coordinate actions and ready the blows that will demolish the forces of the dictatorship."

The FPMR maintained that a paramilitary organization was needed to supplement the military power of the FPMR. The "Rodriguista Militias" had therefore been created to "accentuate the paramilitary preparation and organization of the people." As the link between the guerrillas and the social mobilization process, the Rodriguista Militias answered not to the FPMR but to the Communist party. In addition to serving as the recruiting center for armed troops, the militias acted as the "shock troops" in demonstrations. They promoted disorder and street agitation and generally fomented acts of minor violence.

The Communist party believed that these elements—the party, protests, strikes, the militia, and the armed branch—would together create the conditions to bring down the regime. In November 1984, the FPMR judged the situation to be ripe. The protests had demonstrated that "it is possible to paralyze the country." They therefore concluded that it was time to proceed to a "national mass insurrection" that "would paralyze the country for a prolonged period through a total and ongoing mass mobilization, the city as well as the countryside united in an uprising of all the people."

In truth, this entire perception was nothing more than a delusion stimulated by a faulty theoretical interpretation of revolutionary experiences elsewhere. The unrealistic view of this group is revealed in its rhetoric: "The experience of other peoples demonstrates that it is possible to overthrow powerful military forces.... [T]he people have overthrown powerful armies such as those of the United States in Vietnam, the Shah's army in Iran, Batista's army in Cuba, Somoza's army in Nicaragua."

Three months later, the FPMR's forecast was seconded by the Central Committee of the Communist party, which saw the decisive confrontation coming and predicted the form it would take:

> a general revolt or insurrection of the people, in the course of a national strike and protest day that will immobilize the entire country,...a revolt or insurrection of the masses that will involve the whole population, most of the political and social forces, and, it is hoped, that part of the Armed Forces that opposes the dictatorship. It is a question of a generalized rebellion that will achieve real paralysis of the country: popular uprisings in major urban centers, with the committed participation of the industrial proletariat, students, middle sectors, and peasants. Such actions will be reinforced by effective blows in support of the paralysis that will help accelerate the political and moral crumbling of the repressive forces. The culmination of this process should be the takeover by the masses of the main political centers of the country.[5]

Meanwhile, Pinochet had recovered from the moment of weakness that had led him to open the dialogue in September 1983 and had reasserted his characteristic intransigence. This attitude was expressed in language that was crude and, at times, frankly coarse. In November 1983, the Democratic Alliance announced the first open-air rally in ten years of dictatorship. On the eve of this demonstration, Pinochet defiantly reiterated his unyielding attitude: "The path established by the Constitution is not going to swerve. It will continue straight ahead, although it may displease a group of gentlemen who claim to belong to a former political party [an allusion to the Christian Democrats]."[6] Despite Pinochet's declaration, more than a quarter of a million people attended the demonstration.

Eighteen months later, in July 1985, Pinochet was asked about the possibility of reconciliation and dialogue. He replied, "The word *reconciliation* has many meanings. To reconcile, one must have previously been friends.... It is necessary to proceed carefully because Marxism-Leninism is artful at inverting meanings or creating talismanic words, like *dialogue*, for example."[7]

While the statements by Pinochet and the Communist party became increasingly polarized, Chile was being shaken by acts of extreme poltiical violence. The FPMR's terrorist attacks and assassinations of members of the Armed Forces have already been mentioned. The government's response was no less brutal.

On 30 March 1985, the bodies of three Communist leaders were found on a rural road outside Santiago, their throats slashed. They had been kidnapped from residential neighborhoods several days earlier in a coordinated daylight action by armed contingents. The investigation of these assassinations, like all investigations of crimes against members of the political opposition, produced no results. Nonetheless, on 1 August, four months after the killings, Judge José Cánovas arraigned twelve members of the National Police implicated in these assassinations. The resulting flurry of political maneuvering culminated in General César Mendoza's resigning from both the General Directorship of the National Police (Carabineros) and the Military Junta. This instance was only the second time in almost thirteen years of dictatorship that a member of the Military Junta had stepped down.[8] Pinochet's bald response to accusations against his government was that he would not permit "these problems and difficulties to be used as a pretext to give loose rein to petty politicking and slander against the Armed Forces and Forces of Order."[9]

The policies of the Christian Democratic party had no place in the vicious cycle of violence created by the Communists and the military regime. The Christian Democrats strongly denounced the strategy of the Communist party and the FPMR:

> We maintain that the violent route is, in light of the country's militarization, a genuine crime against the people.... The people suffer repression and terrible material deprivations, and furthermore, in each "confrontation," they risk the loss of their modest dwellings, the telephone booth, the corner store, the community center, or their means of transportation, thus paying a double price in the idiotic and criminal war.... The masses withdraw because in a choice between the familiar violence of the present and the unknown violence to come, they prefer to simply remove themselves from the action. In this way, acts of violence, far from weakening the dictatorship, contribute to perpetuating it.[10]

The difficulty of the moderates' position was illustrated by a published letter from the Christian Democrats to the Political Commission of the Communist Party: "Our party does not wish to be, nor will it be, the civil arbiter of a dirty war between armed groups, to whom would fall the lamentable role of assigning the blame for political crimes, judging the veracity of covert operations of one group or another, or worse yet, certifying the degree of credibility of the contradictory declarations of representatives of armed groups such as the FPMR or the police and the regime's propaganda machine."[11]

After the dialogue failed in 1983, Pinochet traversed the length and breadth of the country reiterating his decision not to negotiate. Meanwhile, the left was becoming increasingly radical. During this period, the Democratic Alliance proposed a four-step transition to democracy: first, Pinochet's resignation and the collapse of the regime; second, the formation of a provisional government; third, the election of a constituent assembly that would approve a new constitution; and finally, the election of a President and national representatives in accordance with the new constitution.[12]

In actuality, this program was not realistic because it did not take into account Pinochet's power. Although the regime had been weakened, it remained stable. The civilian groups that were backing the Democratic Alliance lacked the strength to tip the situation in their favor. Thus the notion that Pinochet could be forced to resign, like most all-or-nothing strategies, immobilized its supporters and cost them time and credibility.

Two years after the creation of the Democratic Alliance in 1983, several indications of change in the Chilean political situation emerged. First, the alliance was becoming increasingly convinced that its program of all-or-nothing transition was not feasible. Second, the Catholic Church was showing renewed interest in seeking a solution to the country's political problems through dialogue and negotiation. Third, sectors of the right wing were distancing themselves from the regime: the National Party (Partido Nacional), was moving closer to the Democratic Alliance, and the National Unity Movement (Movimiento de Unión Nacional) had declared itself independent of both the government and the opposition. In these favorable circumstances, and through the efforts of Sergio Molina (who had been President Frei's minister of finance), eleven parties subscribed to the National Accord for Full Transition to Democracy (Acuerdo Nacional para la Transición Plena a la Democracia) on 25 August 1985.[13]

Unlike the proposal of the Democratic Alliance, this accord did not call for Pinochet's resignation, a provisional government, or a constituent assembly. On the contrary, it declared its acceptance of the Constitution of 1980 in exchange for specified constitutional reforms. The problems presented by this proposal were not simple, however, particularly because the Constitution of 1980 was for all practical purposes, unalterable. Therefore, the first proposed reform of the National Accord was to make the constitution amendable by qualified electoral majorities. The second major proposal was to replace the presidential election that presumably would keep Pinochet in office with free and competitive balloting. Finally, a series of immediate measures were proposed that had been agreed upon by various political groups: ending all states of emergency, establishing electoral registries, recognizing political parties and ending the political recess, approving an electoral law that would provide full democratic guarantees, and ending exile.

The National Accord was clearly a moderate and reasonable proposal. It involved more than a few sacrifices by the democratic opposition, including the major concession of conditional acceptance of the Constitution of 1980. The signing of the accord was met with enormous enthusiasm, but this initiative bore no fruit. As had happened so often before, the politics of the moderates could not withstand the attacks of the Communist party from one side and those of the government from the other.

Pinochet categorically refused to consider any negotiations over the National Accord: "Pseudopolitical cliques have made a great number of people believe that the only system of national salvation is orthodox democracy.... We would be betraying the Chilean people if we were to retreat to the formal and hollow democracy that some politicians aspire to.... It is not a question of intransigence or intolerance but of differences in principles that are not overcome by mutual concessions or by blindly handing matters over to those who want to deceive us."[14] At the end of 1985, in the spirit of Christmas, Juan Cardinal Francisco Fresno, the principal instigator of the National Accord, personally asked the dictator to open negotiations with those who had signed it. Pinochet replied that "it would be better if we just turned the page."

The year 1986 proved to be a difficult one for the opposition. In July national strike days were called by the Civil Assembly (Asamblea de la Civilidad), a coalition of various associations and interest groups, including the truckers' federation, retailers, and professional associations. At this juncture, the country—and perhaps the whole world—was shocked by an appalling crime. On 2 July, two young demonstrators were detained by a military patrol. They were caught carrying a container of paraffin intended to ignite the bonfires that were commonly used to block traffic on protest days. These two young people, Rodrigo Rojas and Carmen Gloria Quintana, were arrested, doused with the paraffin, and set on fire. Rojas, a U.S. resident, had been living in Washington, D.C., with his mother, a Chilean exile who had been savagely tortured by the Chilean police. He died two days after the incident. Quintana survived, but her face and body were permanently scarred by this horrifying act of cruelty. [15]

For the remainder of 1986, Chilean politics jumped beyond the sphere of the Civil Assembly and political parties to the tortured world of weapons, attacks, and the vicious conflict between armed revolutionary groups and government security services. On 12 August, the government announced that it had discovered a clandestine arsenal in an abandoned, almost inaccessible fishing cove in northern Chile. The arsenal contained hundreds of automatic rifles, grenades, and rocket launchers. According to official information, the weapons had been brought into the country by the FPMR with Cuban and Soviet assistance. During the seizure, seven FPMR militants were arrested. In subsequent days, more arsenals were discovered and more Chileans were arrested. The number of confiscated automatic weapons displayed by the government rose to over three thousand, while their alleged value soared to several million dollars.

At first the opposition questioned the veracity of government reports about these incidents. But subsequent discovery of the identity of those arrested, as well as other information gleaned from the leftist parties, made it clear that the Communist party and the FPMR had indeed participated in the operation. The Pinochet regime asked the U.S. government to send a group of experts to examine the arsenals and trace the source of the arms. On 17 September, U.S. Department spokesman Bruce Ammerman indicated that the experts had concluded "that the arms were brought in for the FPMR," that the arsenals comprised "the largest quantity of weapons sent to Latin America clandestinely," and that there was "consistent evidence of external support for Communist terrorist groups."[16]

Twenty-five days after the arsenals were discovered, the FPMR counterattacked. On Sunday, 7 September at 6:40 p.m., Pinochet's motorcade was ambushed. According to the testimony of his guards, Pinochet was returning from one of his vacation homes in the foothills outside Santiago when more than thirty men (who had not even bothered to wear masks) attacked the presidential entourage. Five of Pinochet's bodyguards were killed, and seven were seriously wounded. The dictator, surprisingly, escaped unharmed.

A state of siege was immediately declared. The following night, right-wing paramilitary groups—or perhaps the security services—retaliated. Four activists associated with the extreme left were taken from their homes during the curfew and assassinated at dawn.[17] On 24 October, the security services informed the public that they had detained five of the persons directly responsible for the attack on Pinochet. During the next few days, hundreds were arrested for being associated with the FPMR, the assassination attempt on Pinochet, or the arsenals. Meanwhile, Pinochet welcomed this shift of events into a realm in which he felt more comfortable. The actions of the Communist party and FPMR exemplified the risks cited by the moderate opposition in its rejection of violence. Such activity encouraged "the assumption inside the Armed Forces that the end of the dictatorship would also mean the destruction of the military, the assertion by government allies on the economic and financial right that they should support the dictatorship until the end, and the assertion by the United States and Western Europe that the real choice is between the current dictatorship and a future dictatorship of pro-Soviet character."[18] The assassination attempt and the discovery of the arsenals thus restored Pinochet's position within the Armed Forces to its former strength and also persuaded conservatives, impelled by the fear of communism, to mend their alliance with the regime.

In this atmosphere, political discourse gave way once again to the language of war. Civilian society was demoralized, and the country yielded to a period of lethargy. The resulting political inactivity was prolonged by the arrival of summer and then by preparations for the visit of Pope John Paul II. But by 7 April 1987, when the Pope left Chile, the political situation had undergone a change. In the seven months since the September assassination attempt, the notion had taken hold that the decisive confrontation between Pinochet and the democratic opposition would be an electoral contest. The theme of free elections now began to dominate the debate.

PART II:

The Political Role
of the Chilean Military

CHAPTER 9

The Road to Intervention

By the late 1960s, Chile had the most professional army in South America. More than any other, the Chilean Army embodied the principles of subordination to civilian authority, adherence to military hierarchy, and nonintervention in politics. For forty years, the army's internal structure had remained undisturbed by domestic political disputes or attempts by political parties to enter the barracks in search of support.

This professionalism, however, was gradually destroyed in a process that became evident to the civilian world several years before the 1973 military coup d'état, in the events leading to General Roberto Viaux's failed uprising in 1969. The events that culminated in Viaux's rebellion and the Tacna regiment's being confined to barracks need not be analyzed in detail here. Eyewitness opinions,[1] as well as General Viaux's statements,[2] revealed the incident to have been an obscure military conspiracy carried out by a man who was fiercely ambitious but totally lacking in political judgment. These traits led Viaux to prison and dishonor the following year for participating in the plot that culminated in the kidnapping and death of Army Commander in Chief René Schneider.

Setting aside judgments as to Viaux's motives, it is clear that by 1968-69 politics were being actively debated inside the barracks. Military discipline had weakened, and groups of officers and generals were challenging the principles of subordination to political power and noninvolvement in current political issues. Even more serious was the fact that some officers had begun to question the high command.

These developments are not surprising. Studies of the political role played by the military have shown that military involvement in politics develops precisely when divisions in civilian society become irreconcilable and impede the governmental process. The severe polarization of Chilean society in the late 1960s invited "military arbitration," and the political struggles between 1970 and 1973 proved to be an even greater invitation. Factors specific to the military were also threatening the constitutional order by encouraging criticism of authority, the breakdown of discipline, and political involvement.

Contributing to the crisis that was to explode in the early 1970s was the lack in the Chilean system of any effective means of communication between the civilian and military spheres. Since the 1932 military coup d'état, the Chilean political system had attempted to limit the military to strictly professional duties, assigning it no functions in politics or national development. This approach had created a profound split between civilian and military spheres. The military began to develop a social and cultural life that was completely separate from civilian society. Furthermore, as would be fully demonstrated by the events unleashed in September 1973, military cooperation with the Chilean political system was due not to the assimilation of democratic values but to obedience to a political imperative. Subordination to civilian political authority was accepted as part of an inherited tradition, not as the result of reasoned and firm adherence to principle.

By the end of the 1960s, a profound crisis had emerged in the relationship between political and military authorities. The mutual incomprehension and isolation of civilian and military spheres aggravated the situation because the Chilean governing class remained ignorant of the development and depth of the crisis. Clearly, many Chileans recognized a legitimate desire by the Armed Forces to assume a more important role in national life. But, a realistic agenda for civilian-military relations that could reconcile the demands of the Armed Forces with the exigencies of democracy had not been formulated in intellectual circles or by any political party. Since the modern Chilean political system had been established by the Constitution of 1925, professional frustration had been growing within the Army. By 1968 this military frustration began to manifest itself in serious incidents that threatened or directly affected discipline and the chain of command.

In April 1968, eighty officers studying at the War Academy presented individual letters of resignation, contending that their salaries were not adequate for suitably maintaining their families. As a direct consequence of this event, Minister of Defense Juan de Dios Carmona was replaced by retired General Tulio Marambio. In September of the same year, at the annual Te Deum celebrating Independence Day in the Santiago cathedral, the press reported that a detachment of the "Yungay" regiment failed to arrive in time to pay homage to the President of the republic. This obviously premeditated delay signaled a serious disciplinary problem.

General Carlos Prats refers in his memoirs to the situation in the Chilean Army at the end of 1968 in terms that his contemporaries have confirmed: "On Wednesday morning, 8 October, the routine work of the Annual Assessment Boards (Juntas Calificadoras Anuales) began... at midday I spoke with Generals Cheyre, Carvajal, Mahn, Schneider, Pinochet [apparently Manuel Pinochet], and Camilo Valenzuela, who informed me of the noticeable air of insubordination in the garrison."[3] This progressive breakdown of discipline culminated with the so-called "Tacnazo" on 21 October 1969. General Roberto Viaux, who had recently been retired by a presidential order, took control of the barracks of the important Tacna regiment on the Peruvian border, an act of major insubordination. Moreover, widespread sympathy for Viaux in military circles further eroded military discipline and the command structure.

As a result of these incidents, Sergio Ossa was named minister of defense, General René Schneider was named commander in chief of the Army, and General Carlos Prats became chief of staff of National Defense. Schneider's great gift for leadership and his strength of character temporarily dampened the trend toward political involvement within the Army.

Meanwhile, the 1970 presidential campaign was exacerbating civilian political differences. The constitution stipulated that the candidate receiving one half plus one of the valid votes cast in a universal and direct election would become President. If no candidate received this absolute majority, a joint session of the two branches of Congress would choose between the two candidates who had received the greatest number of votes. Despite the clarity of this constitutional mandate, representatives of two of the three presidential candidates, Jorge Alessandri and Salvador Allende, argued that whichever candidate received a single vote more than the others should be elected President, even if the plurality of votes received fell well below the absolute majority required by the constitution.

Before election day, Alessandri supporters went even further by attempting to block the authority of the Full Congress (Congreso Pleno), to select between the top two candidates. The mixture of optimism and fear prevailing among Alessandri's followers was reflected in an unsigned editorial in the country's leading newspaper, *El Mercurio*: "If the opinion polls are to be believed, the Marxist candidate [Allende] would come in third in the electoral race and the Christian Democrat [Radomiro Tomic] would be second. If, as the polls would have us believe, Mr Alessandri does not receive an absolute majority, then the Congress might choose the Christian Democratic candidate to be President of the Republic, departing from a constitutional tradition that has been applied to those Presidents who did not obtain an absolute majority in the last twenty years, Mr. González Videla, Mr. Ibáñez, and Mr. Alessandri."[4]

The potential crisis prompted *El Mercurio* to put this question directly to Commander in Chief Schneider: "It is possible that none of the candidates will obtain an absolute majority in September. It has been said, with varying overtones, that for the first time the Chilean Congress might not ratify the recipient of the most votes but instead designate the person who obtains the second majority as President of Chile. In that case, what would be the attitude of the Army?"

General Schneider's reply was clear and categorical: "I insist that our doctrine and mission are to respect and uphold the Constitution. According to the Constitution, Congress is authority and sovereign in the case mentioned, and our mission is to assure that its decision is respected." The newspaper countered: "And if that results in a situation of serious internal turmoil that could degenerate into something even worse?" The general replied: "If an irregular situation arises, our obligation is to prevent it from impeding compliance with the Constitution. The Army will guarantee the constitutional verdict."[5]

From the constitutional point of view, the commander in chief's response was unobjectionable. Nevertheless, it intensified the fears of Alessandri supporters and led former presidential candidate Julio Durán to criticize General Schneider bitterly in a lengthy published commentary. Durán said, "I am perplexed by the unusual declarations of the General in Chief [sic] of the Army, Mr. René Schneider."[6]

In the election of 4 September 1970, candidate Salvador Allende received 1,070,334 votes, while his closest rival, Jorge Alessandri, received 1,031,159—36.6 per cent and 34.9 per cent respectively. A sizable contingent of Alessandri supporters then requested that the Full Congress elect Alessandri as President. Meanwhile, it became evident that the Christian Democrats, who held the majority in Congress, were negotiating a vote for Allende if Allende would agree to abide by a Statute of Guarantees (Estatuto de Garantías) to be incorporated into the constitution.

Simultaneously, a military conspiracy designed to block the ratification of Salvador Allende by the full Congress began to develop inside and outside Chile. The activities of the U.S. government toward this end from early September through 24 October 1970 and the direct involvement of President Richard Nixon and the Central Intelligence Agency (CIA) have already been thoroughly documented.[7]

Within Chile, segments of the political right and a group of military officers were involved in an attempted coup that entailed kidnapping the commander in chief of the Army. According to a U.S. Senate report, between 5 and 20 October 1970, the CIA made twenty-one contacts with key military and police officers. It also delivered submachine guns to the group in charge of kidnapping General Schneider.[8] The same

Senate report states: "One of the major obstacles faced by all the military conspirators in Chile was the strong opposition to a coup by the Commander in Chief of the Army, General René Schneider, who insisted the constitutional process be followed. As a result of his strong constitutional stand, the removal of General Schneider became a necessary ingredient in the coup plans of all the Chilean conspirators. Unable to have General Schneider retired or reassigned, the conspirators decided to kidnap him."[9]

That kidnapping ended instead in the assassination of the commander in chief. The death of Schneider made it clear that an unprecedented crisis existed in the Armed Forces. The knowledge that officers had been involved in the plot led to a sense of moral drift, to the impression that something was rotten inside the military institution. After Schneider's death, President Eduardo Frei named General Carlos Prats González, the next in seniority, to succeed Schneider as commander in chief. On 6 November 1970, the newly installed President, Salvador Allende, ratified that appointment.

One consequence of both the "Tacnazo" and Schneider's assassination was the retirement of a large group of generals. When Schneider was appointed, the six generals who were higher on the seniority list (Ramón Valdés, René Sagredo, Emilio Cheyre, Alfredo Carvajal, Alfredo Mahn, and Jorge Rodríguez) were retired from active service. Among them were men of great prestige within the institution. When Carlos Prats assumed office following Schneider's death, four more generals were retired: Camilo Valenzuela, who had been deeply involved in the plot against Schneider, and Generals Francisco Gorigoitía, Eduardo Arriagada, and José Larraín. Thus ten generals were retired in just fourteen months.

If the problems confronting René Schneider on assuming command of the Army had been enormous, those facing Prats were even larger. Tendencies within the military toward political involvement had grown very strong, and support for the idea of bringing down Allende's Popular Unity (Unidad Popular) government was intensifying. The viscerally anticommunist tradition of the Chilean army had begun long before the Russian Revolution in 1917. As has been shown,[10] anticommunism in Chile developed at the beginning of the twentieth century as a result of the conflict between two major European influences: Prussian militarism brought by officers of the Imperial German Army hired to train Chilean soldiers versus the socialist ideas of the Second International, which at that time opposed war, armies, the concept of the nation-state, and the idea of the Fatherland. The Prussian influence was reflected in the *Memorial del Ejército de Chile*, which condemned Bolsheviks and communist ideas at least fifteen years before the Chilean Communist Party was founded in 1922. Thus anticommunism was an established tradition in the Chilean Army long before the right-wing propaganda campaign of the 1960s and early 1970s.

This historical factor was compounded by strong pressure on the military from conservative sectors in Chile who opposed Allende as well as from the U.S government. The intense and even brutal struggles among the various political parties and coalitions were an open invitation to a coup d'état. Conflicts between the judicial and executive branches of the government, and between the legislative majority and the executive branch, only reiterated the invitation to uniformed "arbitration." Finally, some Popular Unity policies also antagonized the military insofar as they threatened the military's monopoly on force by implying that Popular Unity had armed support, an implication that was doubly irresponsible because it was more illusory than real.[11]

Given such adverse circumstances, it is difficult to judge the role of General Carlos Prats. In retrospect, he is one of the most tragic figures of twentieth-century Chilean politics. A professional officer and a faithful representative of an honorable military tradition that stressed noninvolvement in civilian affairs, Prats was nevertheless dragged into the center of the political struggle.

As commander in chief of the Army, Prats had to confront the internal unrest in the Armed Forces caused by provocations from all sides. From the left, pressure on the unity and discipline of the Army came not only from the extreme-left MIR but from large socialist and communist sectors and even from the secretary general of the main party in the government coalition. From the right, command and hierarchy were being undermined by continual calls for military intervention. Within the Army, the tendency toward political involvement was being reinforced by the established tradition of anticommunism and by institutional pressure to ensure respect for the military's monopoly on force, at gunpoint if necessary. From the governmental palace itself, repeated recourse to incorporating of military representatives into the Cabinet ended up being an invitation to the Army to referee politics from above the level of political parties.

General Prats described in his memoirs his experiences during June, July, and August 1973: "I was experiencing the paradox of being a high military officer who proclaimed the doctrine of excluding the Armed Forces from politics but at the same time, on perceiving the sudden turnabout in the domestic situation after a month away, found himself forced to maneuver politically, without the necessary experience in these kinds of conflicts, among political professionals in the government and the opposition. All of this stemming from the strong desire above all to keep his own institution from being dragged into actions that would be fatal to the rule of law."[12]

Troubled by these serious problems, Carlos Prats—more than any of his predecessors—opened the door to formal political involvement of the corps of generals. Faced with difficult and complex political circumstances, he took the unprecedented step of meeting regularly with the corps of generals to discuss such controversial matters as whether the Army should or should not accept the ministerial posts that President Allende was offering, and whether Prats should leave the Cabinet.

Prats's description of the councils of the generals shows a great degree of military involvement in day-to-day politics, an activity that was foreign to the traditional procedures of this group:

Monday, 11 June, I resumed my functions as Commander in Chief, and I had a long meeting with the corps of generals.... I explained my appraisal of the altered domestic situation that I had found on my return [from a trip abroad], and I asked for their opinions. Several generals expressed their points of view. The consensus was that the worst outcome would be military intervention. But there was great concern that governmental inaction on the worsening economic crisis could lead to chaos. I let the suggestion for a solution to the problem come from them, and they proposed exactly what I had been suggesting to the government's politicians.... I committed myself to presenting the argument for the "political truce" as the collective opinion of the generals.[13]

General Prats was aware that this kind of activity by the corps of generals was anomalous and broke with the principles that he himself was committed to defending. He expressly stated: "As was evident, we were in the paradoxical situation that I personally was experiencing: we deliberated about politics (which was constitutionally forbidden), but we were motivated only by the patriotic and sincere desire to prevent the Institution [the Army] from being dragged to the brink of a coup d'état if a democratic formula could not be found."[14]

Given the context of the political and social tensions that were pulling the Chilean system and the Popular Unity government to pieces, political deliberation by the generals and admirals became a policy of the commanders in chief. Some favored the idea of these political discussions, while others, like General Prats, were unable to prevent them and participated in order to channel the discussions toward their own viewpoints on the deteriorating political situation.

The threatening tone that this process gradually acquired is illustrated by Prats's description of the 3 July 1973 session of the corps of generals:

At 1.00 p.m., I met with the generals and explained the disconcerting situation. [A failed military uprising had occurred four days earlier, and President Allende had again asked the Armed Forces to participate in his Cabinet, specifically requesting that General Prats become minister of interior.] Bonilla and Araya suggested that I renounce my position as commander in chief and accept the post of minister of interior as a retired general. I contended that that was not the point because I had no political ambitions, and if I retired, it would be to relax at home. General Araya, who should have been grateful to me, shocked me with his incredible coldness, saying that I had a negative image with the lower officers. I responded that if that was the case, it had come about because the generals had not been faithful interpreters of my professional views.[15]

Before this meeting (on 30 June 1973, the day after the "tancazo"—the attempt to overthrow Allende's government made by an armored regiment in Santiago), General Prats had authorized a delegation of Army generals to meet with their Navy and Air Force counterparts in what was clearly a case of political deliberation. "At midday Admiral Montero and General Ruiz spoke with me and asked me to authorize the participation of several generals in a meeting of generals and admirals requested by the latter to 'orient themselves as to the current situation and standardize policy.' I indicated that I had no problem with that as long as the three commanders in chief were present. At 8.30 p.m., I attended the meeting of five generals and admirals per branch with Montero and Ruiz."[16]

In his memoirs, Prats acknowledged that political discussion was the purpose of these meetings. Prats noted that such meetings "were uncommon in current military practice, given that 'standardized policies' of the three branches were effected daily: in operations, through the assessments of the National Defense staff; in administration through the subsecretaries of the branches; and for overriding issues, through joint sessions of the commanders in chief." Prats stated, "These meetings...were subtly political. I was not mistaken in presuming this, but I thought it would be counterproductive to forbid them in the Army because in addition to demonstrating a lack of trust in the six generals who attended, it would have stimulated clandestine conspiratorial meetings. Since Army Chief of Staff General Pinochet, in whom I had complete faith, attended the meetings, he took responsibility for informing me about any violation of discipline that might occur."[17]

The existence of this Commission of General Officers (Comisión de Oficiales Generales), as it came to be called, was formally expressed in a memorandum that was to be taken to President Allende.[18] According to an interesting article by *El Mercurio* Subdirector Arturo Fontaine and Chief of Information Services Cristián Zegers, the commission began to function on 30 June 1973 and consisted of five generals (or equivalents) from each branch. Fontaine and Zegers describe Pinochet's participation in that meeting in a curious manner: "General Pinochet analyzed the military experience of 29 June and initiated the in-depth discussion by insinuating that political issues should not be addressed there, only economic issues. Perhaps it was not far from the General's intention to approach the burning question that way, without having to sacrifice discipline or the respect owed to their Commander in Chief."[19]

The outcome of this meeting was a memorandum dated 2 July, "based on the suggestions of the Chilean Armed Forces and Navy." Four copies were made, but as Fontaine and Zegers note, "apparently all of them have disappeared." The memorandum contained "twenty-nine points and was an attempt to push Allende toward constitutional requirements: respect for public powers, promulgation of constitutional reform, an end to illegal seizures [of land and factories], suppression of armed groups, and the fulfillment of judicial sentences and other goals necessary for a democratic citizenry to live in peace."[20]

According to my interviews with generals in active service during this period, the Commission of General Officers served as the point of departure for an informal relationship among officers of the three branches, including the option of discussing and exchanging information about a possible military coup. In a recent book, Sergio Arellano Iturriaga calls this group the Committee of Fifteen (Comité de los Quince) because it was made up of five generals from each branch of the Armed Forces. Arellano notes that their meetings became "more frequent and, in order to incorporate other high officers into the conversation, larger sessions were held in private homes. The transition from analysis of current politics to planning a conspiracy was almost imperceptible."[21] These meetings, already beyond the control of the commanders in chief—and without the attendence of General Chief of

Staff Augusto Pinochet—moved to residences in Lo Curro,
La Florida, and other well-to-do areas of Santiago. The
participants progressed from political deliberation to open
discussion of a military coup.

Whatever other significance the Commission of General
Officers may have had, it served from the beginning to
end the isolation of the branches of the Armed Forces by
providing a channel for exchanging information and allowing
the officers to verify that ample backing for a military coup
existed among the various officer corps.

General Prats's command ended with his resignation. This
decision resulted from a deplorable incident that illustrates
how isolated the commander in chief had become from his
generals. A group of Army officers' wives staged a demonstration in front of Prats's house. According to the Military
Intelligence Service (Servicio de Inteligencia Militar), the
wives of at least six generals in active service (Oscar
Bonilla, Sergio Arellano, Raúl Contreras, Sergio Nuño,
Pedro Palacios, and Arturo Viveros) led the group.[22] The
purpose of the demonstration was to deliver a letter, signed
only "Officers' Wives," to Mrs. Sofía Prats. Although meant to
be peaceful, the demonstration became unruly and was broken
up with tear gas by the police. Even more ignominious, a
uniformed officer, Captain Renán Ballas, addressed the crowd,
calling Commander in Chief Prats a traitor to the Army.

Given the seriousness of this incident, General Prats
asked the generals of his branch to sign a declaration
expressing their support. When the majority of the generals
refused to sign, Prats presented his resignation as commander
in chief of the Army and minister of defense, another post
he held at the time.

After Prats's resignation, the post of commander in chief
was passed on to General Augusto Pinochet Ugarte, who
followed Prats in seniority. Relations between Pinochet and
Prats had been excellent during the era of the Popular
Unity government. *El Mercurio* described the relationship in
an article published a year after the military coup: "The
Chief of Staff [General Pinochet] tranquilly awaited his
moment. As an admiral who worked very closely with him
prior to 11 September says, Pinochet always remained calm.

He refused to go along with anything that defied orders or might challenge Army authority. While Prats was in office, General Pinochet cooperated with Prats as required, keeping his misgivings and hopes to himself."[23]

The astuteness (to put it charitably) that General Pinochet displayed in his dealings with President Allende and the Popular Unity government is evidenced in the previously cited article in *El Mercurio*. Fontaine and Zegers allude with reason to the "enigmatic General Pinochet." President Allende

> telephoned the new Commander in Chief, General Augusto Pinochet, after receiving Prats's distressing resignation, and invited Pinochet to dine that evening at his residence on Tomás Moro Street in the company of ten generals. "I have seats for eleven generals, including you," said Allende, and asked Pinochet to select them. This was a way of taking the pulse of the most senior member of the Army after Prats, the enigmatic General Augusto Pinochet Ugarte. Pinochet did not fall into the trap and designated generals whose wives had not participated in the demonstration against Prats.[24]

In fact, Pinochet did not invite any general that Popular Unity considered disaffected to the dinner at Allende's house.

After Prats's resignation, the process of political deliberation which had been going on for some time, accelerated. General Bonilla's post-coup explanation rings true, despite its self congratulatory tone:

> For a long time during this whole process, we in the High Command had been holding our people back. The sergeants, corporals, and soldiers were saying to the captains and to the lieutenants: "Lieutenant, how much longer?" The captains to the majors: "How much longer?" and the colonels, "Well, General, how much longer?" We tried moderation, we tried conciliation on innumerable occasions, twice we joined the government [as members of President Allende's Cabinet] against the will of our institution, forcing it.... Waves of pressure were building from below, not from above.[25]

The debate over who in the military planned and instigated the coup is still unresolved. This issue is politically significant because it affects the issue of legitimacy within the governing group, although less so with the passage of time. Two basic versions have been pieced together as to who authorized the military coup, gleaned from accounts by the most prominent military participants.

One version, formulated after the fact, is that of General Pinochet. Its definitive expression is found in Pinochet's book *El día decisivo* (The Decisive Day). Pinochet says he conceived of the military coup at the moment when he first knew of Salvador Allende's electoral victory on 4 September 1970. According to Pinochet, he met that night with the officers of the Army Sixth Division, of which he was commander. "I told them the following: The people of Chile do not realize the path they have taken. They have been tricked in that they seem to be unaware of where Marxism-Leninism will lead us. Fellow officers, I believe this will be the end of the independent existence of our beloved Chile and that it eventually will become a satellite of Soviet Russia.... This is one of the bitterest nights of my life.... I am at the end of my career. The problem of saving Chile will be left in your hands. May God watch over the destiny of our country."[26]

In actuality, the general was not at the end of his career but at the beginning of its crowning glory. In January of 1971, Pinochet was promoted to Major General. In March of that year, he was transferred to Santiago as chief of garrison for the capital city. In that post, he was in charge of ensuring order for the upcoming midterm election, in which Allende's Popular Unity coalition hoped to achieve a sweeping victory. In early 1972, Pinochet was designated general chief of staff of the Army and from there, according to his account, he organized the military coup: "With great discretion, on 23 June 1972, I issued a circular to eight agencies of the general staff for the purpose of updating certain concepts of our internal security planning."[27]

The final push, according to this explanation, was the designation of General Pinochet as commander in chief of the Army by President Allende himself. "I have often reflected," Pinochet wrote in December 1979, "on why I was the one designated by Allende to be Commander in Chief, in circumstances in which he could have relied on others who were his friends. I had always been openly opposed to the communists.... These are matters of fate. No doubt Allende believed that he was going to manipulate me with his game of small rewards and flattery."[28]

The other version of the origins of the coup, which is based on accounts by contemporaneous Navy, Air Force, and Army officers (all now retired) tends to confirm the complicity of the high command of the Navy and Air Force, with the exception of Admiral Montero of the Navy. This was not the case in the National Police or the Army. In the Army, the instigators and principal organizers of the coup would have been generals with less seniority like the following, whose seniority at the time among twenty-five generals is indicated: Major Generals Manuel Torres (fifth), Ernesto Baeza (sixth), and Oscar Bonilla (seventh); and Brigadier Generals Carlos Forestier (nineteenth), Arturo Viveros (twentieth), Sergio Nuño (twenty-first), Sergio Arellano (twenty-second), and Javier Palacios (twenty-fourth). Within the Army, General Arellano must have played a fundamental role in the conspiracy. Despite the active involvement of Generals Torres and Forestier in the coup itself, their participation in its organization would have been minimal because both were stationed in distant parts of the country, Punta Arenas and Antofagasta respectively.

This listing does not imply that the other generals supported the Popular Unity government. On the contrary, toward the end of Allende's administration, the prevailing sense was that he could count few friends among the generals.

Given this framework, the role played by Pinochet and other Army generals in the coup fits Martin Needler's "swing man" hypothesis, which is based on his analysis of numerous military conspiracies. Needler has posited that the instigators of a coup d'état must put together a decisive coalition of military men who support a coup. In this model, the last man (or group of men) who affiliates with the coup before it is initiated plays a key role, providing the critical margin of support needed for success. Thus the "swing man" is the individual (or group) that tips the balance, whether due to personal influence, public prestige, or (more commonly) his critical position in the chain of command of the armed forces.

The political consequences of this process in the restructuring of power that will result from the coup have been described well by Needler. It is likely that the "swing man," because of his crucial importance for the coup, will be

> placed at the head of the provisional government that emerges after the revolt is successful.... An interesting and paradoxical situation is thus created. The "swing man" becomes the leading figure in the new government; yet he is the person who was least committed to the objectives of the coup...and who was a last-minute addition to the conspiracy perhaps out of sympathy with, or not even aware of, the more fundamental aims of the group that hatched the original plan. Indeed, a situation can actually be created in which the head of the new government actually sympathized with the aims of the conspiracy not at all, but joined it at the last minute only to avoid pitting brother officers against each other, possibly precipitating a civil war.[29]

The fact that General Pinochet and other officers were the group that "tipped the balance" does not entirely belie Pinochet's affirmations in *El día decisivo* about the Army General Staff's internal security preparations. As his book shows, such plans are common. Indeed, every branch of the Chilean National Defense is required to have such plans. General Gustavo Leigh described the situation in the Air Force this way: "The Air Force developed Plan Thunder. But it was a fluid plan, applicable to any political emergency that might arise. We began working on the plan in May or June of 1973. It entailed establishing which units would act in an emergency; their authority, munitions, coordination and communications." When he was asked, "But doesn't that mean you were preparing a coup d'état?," General Leigh replied, "No, because the plan could have been used on behalf of the government as well as against it, or it could have been used to neutralize a confrontation between police and civilians."[30]

The Internal Security Plan (Plan de Seguridad Interior) that Pinochet described was also a "fluid plan," as his book shows. "I made a plan of action. The first step that had to be taken was to gradually transform the defensive posture of the Internal Security Plan into an offensive one."[31] "Defensive" should be understood here as "in defense of the government" and "offensive" as "against the government." The flexible nature of the undertaking is strongly demonstrated by the general's reiteration of its institutional character: "Just before the return of the titular Commander in Chief [Carlos Prats, who was returning from a trip to the Soviet Union and other countries], I issued over my signature an Internal Security Directive from the Commander in Chief of the Army, a document containing the updated Internal Security Plan."[32] After the uprising of an armored regiment on 29 June 1973, the so-called *tancazo*, Pinochet remarked that "the preparation of the revolution practically stopped.... Therefore, after speaking with the director of the War Academy (Academia de Guerra) in early July, I thought it preferable to act openly with the Academy to select a group of trustworthy officers to carry out an 'Evaluation of Internal Order.'"[33]

The "flexible" appearance of these plans must have been perfect: their principal instigator was named commander in chief by the very President whom the plans were designed to overthrow.

The flexible nature of the plan alluded to in *El día decisivo* has been confirmed by examining the statements of high officers and generals who were active during that period. Their information coincides with the following account.

At a generals' meeting in March 1973, it was suggested that existing planning for internal security was obsolete, having been developed in the late 1960s for circumstances that had been overtaken by changing conditions since 1970. Commander in Chief General Carlos Prats ordered the Army staff, which General Pinochet headed, to update internal security planning as quickly as possible. Because metropolitan Santiago was the area needing such a plan most urgently, the Army staff was reinforced with officers from the Santiago garrison. Several generals still in active service participated in this task as majors or lieutenant colonels. The new internal security plan was completed in July of 1973. The chief of the general staff and the newly appointed commander in chief of the Army, General Augusto Pinochet, then arranged a test exercise at the War Academy. Pinochet invited the minister of defense, the generals of the Santiago Army garrison, and President Salvador Allende to this exercise.

All those I interviewed agreed that this plan was applicable to any emergency that might affect Chile's internal security. Thus it is not surprising that the plan was put into effect on 11 September, although it clearly had not been conceived for that specific purpose. There is no reason to doubt that once the "swing men," and especially the commander in chief, had taken sides, the security plan—concealed beneath the garb of a "defensive action" on behalf of the system—could not deliver valuable information for an "offensive" against the government itself.

According to this version of events, General Pinochet's turnaround would have occurred just a few days before the military coup. Pinochet was named commander in chief of the Army on 23 August 1973. At that time or immediately thereafter, he was instructed by President Allende to retire those generals suspected by the government of plotting a military coup. Pinochet has denied making any such commitment to the Popular Unity government. In *El día decisivo*, he recalls that on 24 August, Salvador Allende called to ask that he immediately expedite the resignations of Generals Torres, Bonilla, Carrasco, and Arellano. Pinochet's response was, "Mr. President, it would not be difficult to do what you ask since I have all the Generals' letters of resignation in my desk (I actually lacked two); but if I were to do that, my standing as a man of honor would be undermined from that moment on because it would mean that you named me to this post to effect these resignations, and I won't be a party to that."[34]

General Prats provides a different version of the same incident in his notes for Wednesday, 29 August:

> The Commander in Chief of the Army, General Augusto Pinochet, visited me. He said that he had had some very difficult moments. He had asked the Corps of Generals to give him freedom of action by handing in

their resignations and all did so except for Generals Viveros, Javier Palacios, and Arellano; and since he had said that he would ask that the presidential prerogative [of forced retirement] be applied to them, all the "hard liners" had sided with the malcontents. He added that he now thought he would leave the retirement of the generals pending until October.[35]

A political advisor to President Allende, Joan Garcés, described the events this way two months after the military coup:

> Pinochet, having assumed the post of Commander in Chief, was to call for the retirement—that very week—of six generals suspected of sedition.... Having assumed the position of Commander in Chief,... Pinochet indicated that given the internal situation of the Army, it would be more appropriate to ask just three generals to retire, which he would do the following day. Nevertheless under the pretext that he feared uncontrollable reactions, the Commander in Chief did not expedite the retirement of any of the conspirators.... At the end of August, Pinochet explained to the President the overriding concerns that necessitated deferring the matter until the regular meeting of the Army Assessment Boards, in the second half of September. The retirements would then be presented as an "institutional" procedure carried out by Pinochet as Commander in Chief of the Army. Thus the retirements could not be criticized as "political."[36]

As it happened, the imposed retirement of the generals implicated in organizing a coup never took place at all. According to Garcés's version, the first indication that General Pinochet would be inclined to participate in a future coup surfaced at the meeting of the military high command on Monday afternoon, 27 August, in "an unexpected turn of events. Pinochet stated the need to begin a new phase of collaboration and mutual cooperation, given the difficult conditions within the country; he clearly accepted the possibility of military intervention if circumstances required it, and he recommended tightening coordination of communications among generals and among the branches of the National Defense."[37]

Definitive commitment to the coup would have been made on 8 and 9 September 1973. Sergio Arellano Iturriaga, the son of General Sergio Arellano Stark, describes the events this way:

Saturday the eighth, other Army generals were informed separately. Around 8.30 p.m., my father went to General Pinochet's house to fill him in on the background of the project. Pinochet's reaction was a mixture of surprise and annoyance. When he realized that the only thing needed was his adherence to a decision that had already been made, he seemed overwhelmed. My father told him that General Leigh was at that moment awaiting his call in order to begin coordination. Pinochet asked for a few minutes, promising to call later. For now he needed to reflect. But Leigh never got the call he was waiting for. The morning of Sunday the ninth, Leigh decided to visit Pinochet, but Pinochet was not at home. Leigh went to Pinochet's house again at five in the afternoon and ran into Admirals Sergio Huidobro and Patricio Carvajal and Navy Captain Ariel González, who had brought an agreement to be endorsed by the commanders in chief. Having received no information to the contrary, the admirals concluded that the contact between the chiefs of the Army and Air Force had taken place the previous day. No explanations were provided. General Pinochet stated that he was aware of the plan and that he agreed with it, and he signed it on the spot.[38]

Seven years before Arellano published the above account, General Leigh had detailed an almost identical version to a journalist:

In fact, we made an agreement [he is alluding to an agreement of the commanders in chief and specifically

with General Pinochet] as I have so often repeated, on
9 September, Sunday, at five in the afternoon, when I
went to see General Pinochet at his house, where he
was celebrating the birthday of one of his daughters.
[General Pinochet] was very calm as he listened to my
argument that we could not see the situation reversing
itself. [Pinochet asked,] "What are you planning to do?"
[Leigh answered,] "Because we have gone as far as we
can, I think we are at a point where if we don't do
something, the country will fall into chaos." [General
Pinochet replied,] "Do you realize that this could cost
our lives and many others as well?" "I realize that," I
answered. "Well," he said, "I also believe that the time
to act is near." We were having this conversation when,
without any previous arrangement, Admiral Huidobro,
Admiral Carvajal, and Commander González arrived
with a handwritten note from Admiral Merino that said,
"Augusto, Gustavo, all is lost, if you are in agreement
to act on the eleventh at six in the morning, sign
this paper." And he had signed it. I wrote "Agreed,"
and General Pinochet did too. "If this gets out," said
Pinochet, "it could have grave consequences for us."[39]

On 11 September 1973, the Chilean military overthrew the
political system established by the Constitution of 1925.

As Argentine President Raúl Alfonsín has aptly pointed
out, any seizure of power by the military involves civilians
as well: "The unquestionably military responsibility for the
operational aspect should not make us forget the great civilian
responsibility for planning and ideological support.... A coup
has always reflected a loss of legal sensibility in society and not
just a loss of legal sensiblity in the military."[40] The events in
Chile in 1973 proved no exception to this rule.

Reflecting back over the events described in this chapter,
one can see that the military coup in September 1973 was
actually the third major manifestation of political involvement
by the Chilean Army in the six-year period that led up
to the coup.

CHAPTER 10

The Manipulation
of Military
Professionalism

The previous chapter described the dramatic and contradictory events that led the most professional military in South
America to overthrow its government. That chain of events
was initiated several years before the military coup, by the
increasing political involvement of the Armed Forces. This
involvement eventually undermined military professionalism,
destroyed the principle of subordination to civilian political
rule, and led to the seizure of power and the installation
of what has been most militaristic of the South American
autocracies of this century.

During the first months following the coup, the members of
the Armed Forces felt that they had achieved the full exercise
of political activity, although mechanisms of governing and
political decision making had not yet been established. Surprised by their new position, the leaders of the Chilean
Armed Forces did not realize that once in power, they
could choose among distinct types of military autocracy.
Decisions had to be made about issues involving the duration
of the regime, military professionalism, and the role of the
Armed Forces within the authoritarian political system, the
last issue demanding a choice between political involvement
and noninvolvement.

From September 1973 through the following year, the
military men in government gave the impression of being
equals who spoke freely about political issues concerning
them. They continually reiterated their commitment to

Chilean workers and to social justice. The degree of openness and freedom evidenced in some generals' comments seems inconceivable today.

Rereading Chilean magazines published in late 1973 and early 1974 provides many examples of this openness. Although many statements by officers from all branches of the military were published during that time, only statements by high army officers will be considered here.

As the first example, General Sergio Nuño, vice-president of CORFO (Corporación de Fomento de la Producción), the Chilean state development agency said: "I have experienced up close [while training conscripts] the social injustice of which [the poor] were victims.... Working conditions should be considered as equally important within the business. Arbitrary, unjust, or arrogant treatment should be totally eradicated."[1] Colonel Pedro Ewing, secretary general of the Governing Junta, stated: "Who could oppose increased production, giving land to the people who work it, and worker participation?"[2] General Oscar Bonilla, minister of interior, proclaimed: "Participation is our banner; the Junta is truly obsessed with effecting it at all levels.... A business consists of the person with the money bag and those who help fill it.... The participation of 6 percent of the workers seems like a joke to me. Participation should be not only economic but social.... That is what participation is, and we will ensure that anyone who does not see it that way will be made to see it, whatever it takes."[3]

General Sergio Arellano, commander of the Santiago garrison, described Eduardo Frei, Christian Democratic politican and former President of Chile as "an extraordinary man in his human and intellectual qualities. I ended up becoming friends with him. Frei supporters? No, we are still military men. My way of thinking fits with humanism, and I think that is generally the ideology of the members of the military."[4] A few months later, Arellano observed: "The democratic life that should begin in this country must have a solid foundation that will let us hand over the running of the country to future political parties with absolute security.... Our mission is to help the most underpriviledged classes. We are not going to create new privileges nor are we going to accept the old ones."[5] One last sample from Arellano reads: "We have prevented industry stoppages and reached accords to minimize arbitrariness and injustice.... And it must be recognized that in almost 90 percent of cases, labor is in the right."[6]

General Augusto Lutz, secretary of the Governing Junta, explained: "The takeover was intended to save all Chileans, not to benefit just a few.... The best defenders of the underprivileged classes, of the poor folks of our society, are the four members of the Junta, who always try to favor the needy classes when considering any initiative that might be put forward, whether it concerns salaries, agrarian reform, et cetera."[7] General Washington Carrasco, the intendant of Concepción, offered these reassurances: "Nobody will be persecuted.... I have ordered replacements for agencies without directors strictly by the Army promotion list. We will not make the mistake [made by the Popular Unity government] of being sectarian. There is no doubt that they had an erroneous image of our armed institutions; our discipline is cordial, not authoritarian; it is sympathetic, not classist."[8]

As a final example, General Javier Palacios, who led the assault on La Moneda Palace, proclaimed: "I have been a socialist all my life. I believe that our people need a certain amount of state control, but only in some areas, such as vital services. At the same time, I am a confirmed supporter of free enterprise, and I think private initiative in industry and commerce should be stimulated. I like the Swedish system, although I am convinced that it is never necessary to import any foreign model. Instead, we should create our own."[9]

The confidence and frankness—as well as the ingenuousness—apparent in these declarations suggest that the generals were not aware of the complexities of the political game in which they had become involved. In the years after 1973, when the revolution was taking shape, it began to devour its creators. But in late 1973, the political situation remained largely undefined. The worst part was that the officers then emerging at the political forefront seemed unaware of the necessity of structuring the new reality, which could take many forms. They did not realize that many diverse and even antithetical political systems can come under the rubric of "military regime."

A military junta can be the governing state power that names and removes the chief executive or president at will. A junta can also be subordinate to the military dictator—a second-level political body. Or the president, the supreme state authority, may be named by a civilian electoral body with minority military participation. The first type of military regime has been common in Argentina, the second describes the Chilean military junta after Air Force General Gustavo Leigh's dismissal in 1978, and the third describes the Uruguayan military regime that relinquished power in 1984.

In terms of the personalization of power, some military regimes are identified closely with one person, such as that of Alfredo Stroessner in Paraguay. Other regimes are "dictatorships without a dictator," as occurred in Brazil from 1964 to 1984. A military regime can function in concert with civilian society when existing social currents and political parties are reflected in the army as they are in other social entities. This state of affairs requires an army that engages in political deliberation and that recognizes and respects internal currents of opinion.

Some military autocracies maintain a nominal separation of powers, with the dictator holding executive power and the military junta, or even a predominantly civilian body, exercising legislative power. Such was the arrangement of the Uruguayan dictatorship and its Council of State. Another possible arrangement is to have executive and legislative power wielded by a single person, as occurred in Argentina during General Juan Carlos Onganía's "solitary monarchy."

In some military dictatorships, executive power is separated from military power, with varying degrees of autonomy allowed the president of the republic and the commander in chief of the armed forces. An example is the Onganía government, in which the commander in chief was subordinate to the president. Although the president was named by the military, he could nonetheless remove the commanders in chief at will, a power that Onganía did not hesitate to use. In Brazil, the president of the republic wielded the same authority. The government of General Pinochet exemplifies the opposite case in which both sets of reins are held tightly in the same hand.

Executive power in a military autocracy can reside in a commander in chief, a junta of commanders in chief, or a council of generals. An example of the first is found in contemporary Chile, the second in the recent Argentine military junta, and the third in the Uruguayan military regime. In Uruguay, the Junta of General Officers (Junta de Oficiales Generales), which consisted of generals or their equivalent rank in the three branches, became a kind of "collegial government" in which no single person ranked above the military as a whole. This arrangement led to "a committee game in which the various factions competed, negotiated, compromised, and exercised vetoes."[10] In a military regime, the armed forces may be the key political actor or merely a political instrument. They may discuss and approve policies or simply carry out the orders of the dictator or a nonmilitary oligarchy.

These issues and many others related to defining the new Chilean regime surfaced the very day of the military takeover. In September 1973, and for a long time afterward, the Chilean authoritarian regime was a character in search of an identity. Traditionally in the Chilean military, the commander in chief had dominated the corps of generals, but that tendency was mitigated after the coup because many of the coup leaders were not the most senior officers.

Neither was it inevitable that a government of the Armed Forces would have to become a government of the Army. In 1970 the troop level of the Army (some twelve thousand) was substantially lower than that of the Navy (nearly eighteen thousand). Furthermore, in the years before 1973, a cordial relationship had developed among the three branches of the military and the National Police. Despite institutional differences, they considered themselves to be parts of a single whole—the Armed Forces. In 1973 rivalries of power were still far in the future, as was Army hegemony over the other services, which would eventually subvert the camaraderie of the days of "pure idealism" leading up to 11 September.

When the military first took power in Chile, equilibrium was maintained among the branches of the Armed Forces. For example, the 1974 allocation of cabinent ministries followed a kind of military quota system. Five ministries were assigned to the Army (Interior, Defense, Mining, Transportation, and the General Secretariat of Government), three to the Navy (Foreign Relations, Education, and Housing), three to the Air Force (Public Works, Labor, and Health), and three to the National Police (Justice, Agriculture, and National Resources).

Although any of the various possible types of military autocracy could have been instituted in 1973, the Chilean military regime was heading toward the increasing dominance of the Army and also toward a curious involvement in politics that could be called "distorted professionalism" (*profesionalismo desvirtuado*). This term can be understood to mean (within the the context of a dictatorship) a kind of domination over the Army itself that is based on manipulating a highly evolved professional military tradition and its core values of subordination and obedience to political power, noninvolvement in politics, and discipline and strict hierarchy.

From the moment when Augusto Pinochet began to consolidate his position as Chief of State and Commander in Chief of the Army, the junta's policies exploited the military's traditional values in order to promote a highly personalistic conception of this authoritarian regime. "Distorted professionalism" involves what appear to be the same principles, but they have become perverted in such a way as to lead the military to play an entirely different role within the political system.

One basic requisite of military professionalism is the principle of civilian control—the subordination of the army to civilian political authority. The classic formulation of this concept was developed by Karl von Clausewitz (1780–1831). Since then, it has been adopted by all the professional armies in the world. According to Clausewitz, "War has its own grammar but not its own logic." The logic of war is politics. "War is not merely an act of policy, but a true political instrument, a continuation of political intercourse, carried on with other means.... The political purpose is the end while war is the means of reaching it, and means can never be considered in isolation from their ends.... Policy is the guiding intelligence and war only the instrument, not vice versa. No other possibility exists, then, than to subordinate the military point of view to the political."[11]

The recognition that military science is a field of knowledge with "its own grammar" implies that it is a specialized activity that should be the concern of qualified professionals unhampered by political interference. Political considerations should not influence the careers of officers. But for such a system to be possible, the military must not be called on to participate in political activities. Nor should the military use its monopoly on force to support political factions or projects, whether these originate inside or outside the armed services. Military professionalism is not possible when officers feel that they owe loyalty to various parties or groups seeking to govern. As Samuel Huntington observed, in a society where politics are mixed with military affairs, "the nature of an officer's political loyalties becomes more important to the government than the level of his professional competence."[12]

Military involvement in politics also provokes a loss of institutional cohesion. As one Argentine lieutenant general has noted, the first division within the military occurs between "revolutionaries and antirevolutionaries; then various tendencies emerge among the latter because once they become politicized, nobody can get them to agree; finally, coteries and factions emerge within each branch, or if not that, then rivalries among the three branches, which contribute even more to the destruction of the initial cohesion. In the end, the whole of the country's armed forces become divided into tendencies, factions or parties that represent a veritable cancer in the living organism."[13]

The degradation of the military profession that results from bringing uniformed officers into politics becomes evident to members of the armed forces themselves after they participate in military dictatorships. Testimonies to this effect are a recurring theme in the memoirs and writings of military men. The single dictatorship in Chile prior to the current one, the regime of Carlos Ibáñez del Campo (1927–1931), was judged to have had precisely that effect. Division General Ernesto Medina Fraguela (grandfather of the current General Alejandro Medina Lois) made these revealing comments about the Ibáñez dictatorship after his retirement: "[The Ibáñez government] supported the acquisition of munitions for our artillery,... it improved the barracks and made life better for Army personnel by raising salaries. But Army ethics were trampled by the upper hierarchy, leaving prestige and perquisites to the generals.... It was forgotten that the military serves the interests of the country, regardless of the form of government or the individuals involved in it."[14]

Other evaluations of the enormous damage done during the Ibáñez period to the Chilean army as an institution by mixing military matters with politics were similar. The comments of Vice-Admiral José Toribio Merino (father of the current member of the military junta) are illustrative. One year after the fall of Ibáñez, the man who had been director general of the Navy made these policy suggestions based on his painful experience with the authoritarian regime: locate the Navy organization in Valparaíso, far "from the political atmosphere of Santiago, in order to be able to train professionals without connections or commitments to political parties and their demands.... Organize the Ministry of National Defense under a civilian, a man of laws and codes if possible, who would symbolize the security and stability of the citizens who serve in the armed institutions and would permit them to devote themselves undisturbed to their professional tasks."[15]

Vice-Admiral Merino thus concurs with General Medina, maintaining that although the years following the Ibáñez dictatorship were economically favorable to the military because of the salary increases that he granted, they were nonetheless years of professional bitterness:

> As one of the mild old engineers who left without betraying his profession or ideals described us, we were poor gentlemen. The few years of comfort that followed the military shake-ups did not compensate for the miseries of an entire career. Nevertheless, in the earlier atmosphere of propriety and poverty we had lived calmly, content with the stability and guarantee of the laws and ordinances. And because boundless ambition was nonexistent, professional life was based on a solid ésprit de corps, friendship, camaraderie, and mutual

respect; and the ambitious and the plotters found little room to develop their schemes.[16]

The separation of military affairs from politics and the principle of civilian control are thus essential requirements, the sine qua non of military professionalism. Where these requirements are not met, the military profession is degraded and the army corrupted in spirit and efficacy. Civilian control seems to be the key to all truly effective military systems. In essence, civilian control means not permitting the armed forces to intervene in the political process. It should be noted that the two superpowers, the United States and the Soviet Union, adhere to these principles, as do all democratic governments. Zbigniew Brzezinski and Samuel Huntington, in their celebrated comparison of political power in the United States and the Soviet Union, concluded that "the traditions of military subordination to civil power are deeply ingrained in both Russian and American politics.... The subordination of the military is basic to communist ideology, just as it is to American political beliefs."[17]

The same concern, manifested in a different setting, was part and parcel of the Prussian Army, which served as the inspiration and model for South American military reforms in the late nineteenth and twentieth centuries. The German officer corps upheld as dogma the Clausewitzian conception that "war is an instrument of politics" and that the commander must therefore be subordinate to the politician. The basis of the military professionalism of the German Army in its period of greatest glory, as described by Huntington, was that "the scope of military authority was strictly limited to military affairs. The military played no role in determining domestic economic policies. Foreign policy was the concern of the Chancellor and Foreign Minister. The General Staff stuck strictly to military matters."[18]

Yet the principle of military subordination to political power is ethically acceptable only if it is understood that the army serves the state but does not serve the policies of a particular administration. The army's loyalty must be to the state, not to the transitory holder of power, even if he is the army's commander in chief. But there is more to the difference between true professionalism and "distorted professionalism." Under distorted professionalism, in the name of subordinating the military to political power, the army is linked to a specific government and its day-to-day policies.

The fall of the German Army from military glory to moral and professional ruin paralleled its path from subordination to the state to submission to Hitler's dictatorship and its policies. Andreas Dorpalen, noted analyst of civic-military relations during the Third Reich, has observed: "The question has often been raised as to why the generals submitted to [Hitler's] influence, particularly after they realized that the war was lost in military terms. Trained in obedience and discipline, European generals are not like those in Latin America or the Near East; they seldom rebel against their own governments, however brutal the government's actions might be."[19]

When the basic distinction between state and government is blurred, the military becomes subject to a painful contradiction. At the same time that its "apoliticism" is being affirmed, the military is being used to support the government's policies. In Chile the trend toward distorted professionalism was expressed along two basic lines. The first was Pinochet's establishing his dominance over the other members of the junta and the Army's dominance over the other branches of the military. The second was his establishing complete political control over the Army. The Army was simultaneously pulled out of politics and transformed into an obedient and nondeliberative instrument of the policies initiated by Pinochet as Commander in Chief. Thus the regime policy changed from its initial rhetoric of democratic restoration to that of an open-ended military exercise of power, justified by what the military regarded as the incapacity of civilians to govern.

Yet at the same time, the Army was being progressively distanced from political power and transformed into a political tool. In effect, in the name of military professionalism and propriety, the Armed Forces were being denied the right to deliberate over governmental matters while being used as the instrument to execute the regime's policies. In these ways, the concept of "government of the Armed Forces" has been redefined in contradictory terms. Chile has a government of the Armed Forces in the sense that the military provides the force that is the regime's principal (and at times, only) effective support. But it is the Commander in Chief of the Army who governs in the name of the Armed Forces. The Chilean regime is not a government of the Armed Forces in that the military has neither authority nor responsibility for determining policy. This exclusion of the military from any political participation is justified by the classic principles that were adhered to by the Chilean Army in democratic periods—subordination to political authority, obedience, and noninvolvement in politics.

Thus the Chilean Armed Forces have followed a contradictory path. Under democratic rule, the Armed Forces were professional, obedient, and apolitical—subject to legitimate civilian political control and remaining above political disputes. But divisions within the civilian world corroded the governmental system in the early 1970s, and the Armed Forces were gradually transformed into a political force.

In order to fulfill this role, the Armed Forces had to begin to discuss, elaborate, and determine policy. But that situation lasted only a short time. Power was snatched from the generals, and under Pinochet, the Army was restored to the bases of nondeliberation and obedience to political power. The difference was that this time the Army found itself committed to support and defend a particular set of policies. The Army thus changed from a political actor into a political instrument; it is now the "apolitical servant" of the regime's policies.

Political involvement and noninvolvement have both served a purpose within the authoritarian regime. The shift to military involvement opened the way for the military coup. Afterward, the re-establishment of military noninvolvement in politics served to consolidate the authoritarian regime and concentrate political power in the person of the Commander in Chief. It is therefore not surprising that after the military coup of 1973, the process of active political deliberation was rapidly reversed by a systematic policy of the commanders in chief, especially General Pinochet.

"Apoliticism," now elevated to the preeminent position among the principles of professionalism, has been emphasized time and again by the commanders in chief. For example, General Nilo Floody, inspector general of the Army, stated: "The Armed Forces have not become politicized. They are as professional as former armies were. At one moment, a general or an officer may perform government tasks and the next day perform tasks within the Army. An officer understands this difference. That is why we military men are not involved in politics. It is the government that elaborates economic, and social policies, etc.... It would be dangerous if we were all expressing opinions and being politically active, but that is not the case."[20]

General Washington Carrasco, vice-commander in chief of the Army, observed: "Our system is totally different from the type that has predominated in countries with military governments. The President of the Republic has been extraordinarily visionary in not politicizing the Armed Forces. Basically, they attend to their professional military duties."[21] The same sentiments have been expressed by Lieutenant General Julio Canessa, vice-commander in chief of the Army: "Neither the Army nor the Navy has ever been politicized. We have always been apolitical, and we are continuing along the same line."[22] Finally, General of the National Police René Peri answered a journalist's question about his political viewpoint: "I have been in the National Police since I was nineteen years old, and we do not have a political viewpoint."[23]

Yet at the same time, the Armed Forces were declaring that they perceived no contradiction between professional political neutrality and the practical fact that they were backing and effectively supporting a particular government and its policies. According to Lieutenant General Canessa: "The fact that we consider ourselves members of the military government does not mean the Army is politicized. I think we have never experienced a period of stronger professionalism.... [W]e have contributed a measure of dedication to the tasks of government, considering them one more service that all professional soldiers can and should, if so ordered, render to their country in an emergency. That is why I do not think there is any danger of politicization of the Army."[24] Canessa later reiterated: "I want to make it clear that although the Chilean Army identifies with its government, it has not become politicized or lost the military virtues that have always characterized it. Today we have the healthy ambition to become a better military, more professional than ever."[25] And again, "The Chilean Army currently enjoys a high degree of professional efficiency because although it clearly identifies with its government, it has not become politicized in these last ten years, nor has it lost the military virtues that have always characterized it."[26]

Another fundamental element of military professionalism—obedience—has become the basis for supporting policies that are neither discussed nor ratified by members of the military. General Fernando Matthei, commander in chief of the Air Force asserted: "I am sure that there are many people [in the Air Force] who think differently than I do. Probably each one of the nine thousand thinks differently. But I have no doubt that any order of mine—and I am not going to give orders that are not legitimate—will be instantly obeyed. I can guarantee that, but I do not require anyone to think the way I do."[27] Obedience has also been extolled by Vice-Admiral Raúl López: "[The Armed Forces] are still—and I am speaking mainly about what I am familiar with, the Navy—an essentially professional body where the principles of nondeliberation, hierarchy, and discipline are maintained absolutely the same as always.... [F]rom the beginning, *one* authority was established. And behind that authority lies the absolute cohesion of the Armed Forces that back it."[28]

Supporting policies on the basis of obedience and not on the basis of debate and political convictions has the important effect, in the judgment of the military, of preventing the "political deterioration of the Armed Forces." On this subject, General Sergio Badiola commented: "It does not worry me [that the Armed Forces might be weakened by being in power]: vulnerability comes from politicization, and the Armed Forces and the Forces of Order have not become politicized."[29] Vice-Admiral Raúl López insisted that the Armed Forces "will not become weaker in the government—they do not participate in political debate or in political tasks as an institution."[30]

After the regime imposed the Constitution of 1980, the criteria of obedience and political noninvolvement led to a revival, within the context of the dictatorship, of the old idea of a constitutionalist army. Lieutenant General Julio Canessa expressed this idea:

> The Chilean Army has always been completely obedient to the Constitution and, naturally, they are to this Constitution of 1980, which was approved by an overwhelming majority, even its transitional articles. What is essential is subordination to the Constitution, assuring compliance, and the Army will always do that.... The Army, as part of the Armed Forces, has a clear role in the Constitution and in the new institutionality, which requires it to be apolitical and professional. This means staying outside political party struggles. The Army will always have the legally constituted government as interlocutor; in no case will it make deals with political parties.[31]

In addition to this emphasis on constitutionality, manifestations of a strengthened hierarchy and enforced obedience became more frequent after 1976. This trend contrasted with the initial period of the military government, when the generals' references to the Commander in Chief had indicated closer and more equal personal relations. Lieutenant General Canessa stated that The Armed Forces "are hierarchies, with chains of command in which the most senior officer, in this case the Commander in Chief, is in charge and is responsible for everything."[32] This view was seconded by Colonel Ramírez, vice-president of CORFO, the Chilean national development agency: "Not a piece of paper moves in the government if he [Pinochet] does not move it. Not only in the Ministry of Economics, but also in internal and external political, economic, and social matters."[33]

Thus by basing their discourse on the traditional values of professionalism, the Chilean Armed Forces had created the illusion of having returned to the point of departure, of having reconstructed military professionalism. In appearance, they certainly occupy their traditional position—apolitical, subject to control by civilian political power, hierarchical. But true military professionalism involves more than the mechanical observation of these tenets. Indeed, once these principles are removed from a legal and ethical framework, they can become the absolute ruin of the army as an institution.

Is subordination to political power equally valid when the source of power is a Hitler or a socialist dictator rather than a government based on the rule of law? Does political neutrality refer only to those matters that concern the military profession (given the Clausewitzian principle of the subordination of war to politics), or are members of the armed forces also expected to forgo personal opinion and subscribe to a set of orthodox beliefs about politics, economics, recent history, and the social order? How can a professional soldier maintain his dignity and his conscience in the conflict among obedience, morality, and the law? How can political neutrality be made compatible with the duty to be the armed executor of certain policies?

In nineteenth-century professional armies, such problems did not seem to arise. More precisely, they were obscured by the greater simplicity of war and, above all, by the presence of more or less benevolent dynasties in political power. But surely professionalism has never been a matter of mechanical adherence to principles that are not values in themselves. The German Army—one of the most professional in the world—was destroyed through abuse of the concepts of obedience and political neutrality. A mixture of naiveté and political malformation led the Wehrmacht to assume the "purely professional" role of serving as an instrument of violence.

Most of the statements by Chilean generals cited here as illustrations of "distorted professionalism" were made between 1980 and 1983. To any observer of military affairs, these statements must seem grotesquely exaggerated in their straining to the limits the concepts of obedience, hierarchy, and submission to political power. Nevertheless, the Chilean regime once again seems destined to disregard any sense of moderation.

In October 1985, Lieutenant General Raúl Benavides was removed from his post as presidential representative to the

Military Junta. It was rumored that Benavides had privately voiced concerns to Pinochet about the slow implementation of the political provisions of the Constitution of 1980. Six years beyond the age of retirement, Benavides had remained in the service by means of special presidential dispensation. Thus as a direct consequence of his removal from the junta, he was retired from active duty. Benavides was the last Army general other than Pinochet who had held the rank of general at the time of the military coup; after Benavides's departure, no one remained who had ever dealt with Pinochet informally and as an equal.

Lieutenant General Julio Canessa succeeded Benavides as Pinochet's representative to the Military Junta. Formerly vice-commander in chief of the Army, Canessa was also past due to retire and still in the service through Pinochet's discretionary measures. Canessa's relationship with Pinochet was in no way that of an equal, however; he was instead an obsequious and submissive subordinate. Two revealing public statements illustrate the nature of this relationship. On the eleventh anniversary of Pinochet's selection as Commander in Chief, Canessa enthused: "General, it is not common for subordinates to openly express their evaluation of the work of their superiors, but it is not forbidden to pay homage out of respect, loyalty, and gratitude."[34] A year later, when a journalist asked Canessa if he and Pinochet were good friends, Canessa again expressed extraordinary deference. His statement is especially revealing considering that he was second in command to Pinochet in the military hierarchy: "Let us clarify things. I have known General Pinochet for forty-three years, since I was a recruit and he was the lieutenant instructor of the company where I was a cadet. I knew him well as a subordinate, and it is not customary in the Army for a subordinate to say that he is friends with a superior."[35]

When Canessa became a member of the Military Junta in October 1985, the post of vice-commander in chief was offered to General Santiago Sinclair, who had worked in the goverment's Moneda Palace for the previous six years, in close proximity to the President. By this time, Sinclair had considerably more seniority than the other ministers in

Pinochet's Cabinet. In 1979 Sinclair had been designated as the President's chief of staff, a position with ministerial status. It later became the basis for establishing the Ministry of the Secretary General of the President (Minsterio Secretaría General de la Presidencia), which has been headed by a military officer since its inception. The office was created to apply the principles of bureaucratic management as used in the military to political matters. Thus the "President of the Republic-Commander in Chief" has two general staffs: one for analyzing military problems and the other for analyzing political problems.

With Sinclair as vice-commander in chief, the rhetoric of obedience and submission to the Commander in Chief reached levels that surpassed even the subordination of the German military to Hitler. At a military ceremony on the thirteenth anniversary of Pinochet's appointment as Commander in Chief of the Army, Sinclair spoke for the Army in an astonishing address to several thousand soldiers in attendance. This speech consisted of deifying Command (with a capital C) and asserting the embodiment of Command in the person of Augusto Pinochet. Sinclair explained that Command is the quintessence of everything miliary and at the same time a moral absolute that presupposes infallibility. Command leadership may only be obeyed, never opposed. Pinochet is the figure in which this infallible military and moral absolute resides incarnate. Pinochet is soldier and politician, military leader and statesman, to whom "his" Army (Sinclair used the possessive) renews its loyalty and obedience beneath the gaze of the Mother of God.

Nothing is more noble and sublime than Command because its objective is nothing less than the defense of the Fatherland. Command is voice, conscience, justice, and it is ennobled by the commitment and personal example of the one who wields it. Command guides spirits and unites wills, carrying them to success in endeavors that often require supreme heroism. In you, First Soldier of the Republic, we see the wise leader, the Commander who has been able to illuminate the difficult paths of these years. In support of the high office of that Command, you will find your soldiers always ready to triumph and to offer their lives if the defense of the Fatherland so requires.

...

You have had but one ambition: the greatness of Chile. A single motto: "Duty is above question."... And so, my General, we wish to publicly renew our obedience and loyalty to the inspiration of the hierarchical authority of Command and the moral authority that flows from your position as military leader.... Providence willed that you carry the torch of the pledge that we make to the Fatherland; thus, our loyalty is loyalty to Chile.

...

Beneath the gaze of the Mother of God... I repeat, beneath her gaze, and with the sacred inspiration of God and country, the Army of Chile acts with a profound and undeniable sense of justice to demonstrate before the citizenry the recognition and honor owed the first soldier of the Republic, Captain General Augusto Pinochet Ugarte."[36]

Fifteen days later, in the message sent by the corps of generals to Pinochet after the attack that almost cost his life, Lieutenant General Sinclair articulated what would appear to be the logical culmination of his vision of Command—the image of the Commander in Chief as sacred: "My General, the sacred figure of our Commander in Chief has been the victim of an assassination attempt. The Army repudiates, condemns, and will not forgive this act."[37]

In the next part of this book, I will analyze certain internal elements of the military institution that the "President of the Republic–Commander in Chief" has used to establish domination over the Armed Forces. Pinochet's dominance has increased to the point that his power has no counterweight. It is especially strong over his own branch of the military, the Army.

119

PART III

Controlling
the Chilean Army

CHAPTER 11

The Consolidation
of Authority

As has been discussed, the principle of civilian control is a prerequisite for military professionalism and efficiency. In terms of governmental structure, civilian control requires that political and military functions be separate and that the latter be subordinate to the former. Political leadership belongs to the chief of state. Military leadership, on the other hand, is most fittingly vested in a professional officer. The legitimacy of the chief of state is based on political criteria, while the legitimacy of military leadership is based on technical and bureaucratic skills.

The nation's highest military title is often assigned to the political leader as a manifestation of the principle of civilian control over the military. The chief of state may serve as titular commander in chief or, as was the case in democratic Chile, as generalissimo of the armed forces. In any case, such titles refer to political control. While the traditional title for the highest military office in Chile has been commander in chief, other countries have favored such titles as inspector general or general army chief of staff to emphasize the professional and technical nature of the position.

Separating political and military power has another justification. Precisely because the military is a hierarchical, obedient, nonpolitical body, it can be most dangerously affected by an excessive concentration of power. The traditional military values of institutional hierarchy and obedience render the military defenseless against abuse of power. Service members as well as military organizations are vulnerable because their institutions are based on rigid discipline and obedience, themes that recur throughout military literature. As a professor of military and political history at the U.S. Air Force Academy has observed:

> Power does tend to corrupt, and throughout history military men have had no special immunity to what Will Durant aptly calls the "poison of power."... Indeed, the military commander rarely tolerates adverse comments from any subordinate.... It is no accident [that the military] clings tenaciously to a system whereby a sterling career may be ruined by the single adverse rating of a superior. Moreover, the system instinctively protects itself by strongly discouraging admission of error, particularly serious error. The powerful, in other words, not only make mistakes but can dictate cover-up mistakes.[1]

For these reasons, the countries that best foster the development and efficiency of their armed forces not only separate the leadership of the state from supreme military authority but limit and distribute military power. For example, during the reign of Kaiser Wilhelm, Germany's period of greatest military glory, military authority was divided between "the army and navy and then further subdivided within each service." Samuel Huntington has detailed this subdivision:

> Each had a tripartite headquarters organization consisting of: (1) a ministry, normally headed by a professional officer, and concerned with the administrative, political, and logistical aspects of the service; (2) a cabinet, also headed by an officer, and occupied with personnel matters; and (3) a staff, devoted to the planning of military operations. None of these headquarters had command authority over the fleets and army corps,...all reported directly to the Kaiser, who was thus able to pick and choose from the military advice offered him. In addition, there was considerable rivalry in the army among the War Ministry, the Military Cabinet, and the General Staff.... The effects of the limited scope and multiplicity of military authority were counterbalanced

by the high level of that authority. All the top military leaders had the right of direct access (*Immediatstellung*) to the Kaiser as Supreme War Lord which weakened vertical controls over the military.[2]

A military dictatorship—in its efforts to survive over the long term—tends to confuse the two roles. The positions of chief of state and commander in chief of the army tend to be consolidated in a single person. In most cases, the highest military authority will likely have sole control and unlimited powers. But this fusion of the two posts leads to the breakdown of the basic parameters of military professionalism, as history has shown. In the first place, such fusion involves the army deeply in daily politics and party disputes. Affiliated with the commander in chief, who is also the political leader of the nation, the army no longer fulfills a technical function within society but is transformed into an armed guardian of government policies. This change in function inevitably has repercussions on the careers, promotions, and retirement of officers. Political and personal loyalty to the chief of state and his policies assume priority over criteria of professional merit and seniority.

Evidence of the foregoing has led some South American military regimes to revert to trying to keep the two positions separate. In doing so, the armed forces seek to achieve political and military objectives that are not attainable when the same person occupies both posts. One political objective is to avoid the personalization of power, that is, to prevent the dictatorship installed by the military from becoming independent. In a military regime, the argument goes, the institutional power—the armed forces—should be able to limit the power of the individual serving as commander in chief at any given time. By separating the positions of commander in chief and president, the military also seeks to shield officers and troops from manipulation through extraprofessional pressures that would be exerted by a consolidated personal dictatorship. For these reasons, the recent military dictatorships in Argentina, Brazil, and Uruguay all deliberately separated the posts of president and commander in chief.

Of the three, Argentina has experienced the greatest number of military governments and regime types within those military governments. Several forms of relationship between Argentine chiefs of state and commanders in chief will be examined here.

The dictatorship of Juan Carlos Onganía (1966–1970) has been called a "solitary monarchy." Unlike many other military leaders, Onganía believed that the army should stay out of politics. During the military coup that installed him, he insisted on complete respect for the principles of hierarchy, obedience, submission to political power, and noninvolvement in politics, the last referring to separating the positions of president and commander in chief.

As Alain Rouquié has noted, the Argentine revolution of 1966–1970 "was presented as a military regime, although the army as an institution did not retain power."[3] The joint commanders in chief who effected the military coup of 28 June 1966 immediately designated retired General Onganía as President of Argentina. The junta then dissolved itself. Onganía assumed all executive and legislative powers as well as control over the military apparatus.

In December 1966, significant differences emerged between Onganía and General Pascual Pistarini, the commander in chief and author of the coup. Onganía proceeded to order Pistarini into retirement and replaced him with General Julio Alsogaray. Twenty months later, in August 1968, new disagreements led to Alsogaray's being ousted and replaced by Alfredo Lanusse. These changes reflected Onganía's belief that "the armed forces do not govern or cogovern but constitute the backing for the Argentine Revolution."[4]

Nevertheless, Onganía as President never wielded absolute power over the Argentine Army. He did not have complete control over military appointments nor could he "assemble a wholly satisfactory staff. Tradition, the distribution of power, and the obliteration of political divisions resulting from the 'blue phenomenon' [the legalist faction of the military] and from revolutionary confluences combined to prevent the creation of an Onganista army."[5]

When General Onganía was overthrown by his own comrades in arms in 1970, the new military junta designated

General Roberto Marcelo Levingston as President of Argentina. This time, however, the junta declined to dissolve itself and decided to keep the new chief of state under its direction, specifying that he should consult the junta on "all important matters." Later, yet another form of relationship between the Argentine chief of state and the military junta was established. Under this arrangement, the military junta acted as the highest political entity. A scholar writing at the time observed that the junta

> nominates and removes the President of the Republic, exercises final political control, and tacitly retains constituent authority unto itself. The commanders in chief individually continue to command the armed forces and security forces and have the final say on promotions and transfers within their respective branches. The President of the nation holds all the powers that the Constitution assigns to that office, with the exception of military command. Furthermore, he holds the powers of the Congress, which he shares with an agency made up of officers of the three branches of the armed forces that has the power to advise and consent.[6]

In exceptional circumstances, the Argentine military junta could grant a special concession to the commander in chief of the army, authorizing him to retain the dual position of president of the republic and commander in chief. But that was a provisional status, revocable at the will of the junta. This arrangement was called the recourse to a "fourth man," a power structure that added one more to "the three" of the military junta. The fourth party was the president of the republic, a retired general.

The problems posed by consolidating the posts of commander in chief and president of the republic were analyzed by Argentine General Roberto Viola in an interview he granted a Chilean journalist while awaiting nomination by the military junta to succeed General Jorge Rafael Videla as chief of state. At that time (October 1980), Viola indicated that the reasons for separating the two positions were "purely doctrinaire" and represented the search for "a political system with counterweights of power to balance and stabilize it. For that reason,...the structure...in which the President does not occupy the post of Commander in Chief was created. There are other practical objectives,...among them the depersonalization [of military power]."[7]

Viola later added that in order to avoid concentration and personalization of power, the length of time that one person could hold both posts was limited to "a maximum of three years.... I want to point out that in the Army, the tenure [of commander in chief] is limited to two years. After that period, the outgoing commander designates his successor. Thus the composition of the Military Junta changes regularly."[8]

In Uruguay, as in Argentina, the military regime's power structure distinguished between the military junta, the commanders of the armed forces, and the president of the republic. During the eleven years of military rule (1973–1984), two civilians and one retired general served as president. The president held executive power but had no authority in military matters, and his position was always precarious vis-à-vis the power of the armed forces. The fundamental explanation for the fall of President Juan María Bordaberry in 1976 was that Bordaberry wanted to use the military to buttress his regime but would grant it no say in the regime's political conduct. In that sense, Uruguayan military institutions always controlled the political direction of the regime, in contrast with their Argentine counterparts under Onganía and particularly with the Chileans under Pinochet.

Seeking to maintain that control, the Uruguayan Armed Forces created an institutional framework for their regime that targeted three objectives: first, to separate the posts of president and commander in chief; second, to prevent by means of forced retirement any personalization of the office of commander in chief; and third, to place military power in what Juan Rial has called a "governing college" (colegiado gobernante) made up of all Army and Air Force generals and Navy admirals. The Uruguayan military decision-making body was never a single chief of state or a commander in chief placed above the armed forces but rather "the totality of the hierarchy of superior rank."[9] Beginning in 1976, the Uruguayan presidential election was turned over to the

Council of the Nation (Consejo de la Nación), a new agency made up of the members of the Council of State (Consejo de Estado)—all of them civilians—and the members of the Junta of General Officers. The presidential nomination required the agreement of two-thirds of the members of this council.

The case of the Brazilian military dictatorship (1964–1984) is distinct from those in Argentina and Uruguay. In Brazil the armed forces retained the decisive role in nominating the presidential candidate, whose selection was then approved by an electoral college composed of the members of the National Congress and the delegates of state legislative assemblies. Until the 1984 election of Tancredo Neves, this nomination always went to a retired general. Once the designation was made, the Brazilian president wielded powers characteristic of a mature political system. As supreme commander in chief of the armed forces, the president named and removed the military commanders in chief and directed defense policies.[11] The armed forces, as mandated by the Brazilian Constitution, were established as national institutions organized on the basis of hierarchy and discipline and subject to the president's authority.

The 1977 conflict over presidential succession between General João Baptista Figueiredo and Minister of the Army General Sylvio Frota demonstrated that these constitutional provisions were followed. When Figueiredo was nominated president by the chief of state, retired General Ernesto Geisel, Minister of the Army Frota protested, charging that the Brazilian Armed Forces had been excluded from the process of presidential succession and had suffered a serious erosion of political power. Geisel's response was to decree the dismissal and retirement of the contentious minister of the army.[12]

Nothing resembling these events in Brazil has ever occurred in Chile, where General Pinochet has taken on the functions of both chief of state and commander in chief. On 19 August 1977, the Chilean Military Junta created the post of vice-commander in chief. By virtue of this initiative, the commanders in chief "may delegate, by internal order, part of their institutional powers to the institutional general chiefs of staff or to the general officer who is next in seniority in the institutional line of command."[13]

In reality, the only commander in chief who has actually exercised this power is General Pinochet. The significance of the new position of vice-commander in chief was aptly explained by one of its incumbents. General Washington Carrasco stated that the post was created because it is not possible for General Pinochet

> to attend to all the problems of the institution while attending to those of the country. Therefore President Pinochet decided to delegate part of his powers to a vice-commander, maintaining, of course, control of command.... He retains all authority relative to appointments to the High Command, decisions related to planning and organic restructuring of the institution. But all the rest is the direct responsibility of the vice-commander, who has the great responsibility of answering to the Commander in Chief as to the progress of the Army under his delegated authority.[14]

Thus the position of vice-commander in chief is characterized by its precariousness. It may exist—or be revoked—solely according to the wishes of the Commander in Chief, and it lacks the most important powers of command.

CHAPTER 12

Bending the
Retirement Rules

Before 1973 the Chilean military, like most professional armies, was subject to regulations that based the rules for retirement of officers and commanders in chief on seniority. These provisions prescribed mandatory retirement for all officers "who had fulfilled thirty-eight years of service as officers, or forty effective years toward retirement. Nevertheless, the President of the Republic may refuse to accept retirement applications from officers who are acting as commanders in chief or chiefs of staff of National Defense and may keep them in service for up to three additional years."[1]

There were many justifications for these regulations. It did not seem prudent for one person to remain in a position of such preeminence and power as commander in chief for an extended period. Such a situation could threaten the balance of power within the government by enabling the commander in chief to gain dominance over other officials, including the president. But this risk is not limited to democratic systems, as experience has demonstrated in the military regimes of the Southern Cone of South America. Therefore, the commanders in chief in the military dictatorships of Brazil, Argentina, and Uruguay were made subject to rules governing retirement by seniority.

In a military regime, the absence of regulations for mandatory retirement can lead to the personalization of army leadership, which could threaten officers' careers and the military institution itself. The formal and informal influence of the commander in chief over the promotion and retirement of his colleagues is so great that its prolonged exercise by the same person creates the possibility that a corps of generals and other ranking officers could be selected more on the bases of personal loyalty and friendship than according to military merit. This approach would obviously bankrupt the principle of military professionalism.

Furthermore, the long incumbency of a commander in chief at the head of a corps of generals characterized by constant turnover inevitably creates a wide gap in age, experience, and influence between the commander and his generals. This disparity undermines the basis of collaboration essential to managing a large bureaucracy such as the armed forces. Within society's most hierarchical institution, the army, it is difficult to imagine a frank exchange of views between a commander in chief and a general twenty years his junior, who owes his career in part to the commander and who was only a new captain or major when his commander was already a general.

In Chile military retirement rules were partially revoked on the last working day of 1976, when two decrees were promulgated. Decree-Law 1639 established exemption from mandatory retirement by seniority for any high officer who was "carrying out...government functions specified by the President of the Republic by means of supreme decree."[2] This decree-law strengthened General Pinochet's position over the generals of not only his branch but all the Armed Forces. By virtue of this decree, generals who ordinarily would have been obligated to retire because of seniority could remain in their posts as long as the President so directed. Thus the utter dependence of the positions of these high-ranking officers was institutionalized in a form that exists to this day.

On 19 September 1978, a Command Order allowed the title of lieutenant general of the Army to be conferred on division generals who were serving past retirement. It is interesting to note that some of the highest positions in the military hierarchy have shared this rank and its intrinsic insecurity.

On 20 September 1978, three officers, who had completed forty-one years of service but remained in active service because they were carrying out government functions, were named as lieutenant generals. They were Generals Herman Brady Roche, president of the National Energy Commission

(Comisión Nacional de Energía); Raúl Benavides Escobar, minister of national defense; and Carlos Forestier Haengsten, vice-commander in chief of the Army.[3]

The Constitution of 1980 allowed General Pinochet to appoint a replacement member to the Military Junta. Transitional Article 14 authorized him to designate "in his place, as titular member [of the junta], that general who follows him in seniority." But this designation was also conditional because the constitution indicated that "the President of the Republic may replace said member at any time with another general officer of his institution, following the order of seniority."

In March 1981, General Raúl Benavides, who by then had served more than three years in the insecure rank of lieutenant general, was appointed to the junta. The three Army generals who have served as minister of defense since 1978—Benavides, Carlos Forestier, and Washington Carrasco—also served as lieutenant generals.

Finally, General Julio Canessa was named vice-commander in chief of the Army immediately before his prescribed retirement. This designation by General Pinochet was communicated to him on 6 October 1981. Shortly thereafter, Canessa declared to the press his profound gratitude to the Chief of State: "On 31 December 1981, I will complete thirty-eight years as an officer, and on 30 March 1982, forty years of service. According to the regulations, I should be obligated to retire. Nevertheless, through the provision establishing the rank of lieutenant general, the Commander in Chief of the Army can direct a major general in those circumstances to continue in service, carrying out extrainstitutional missions or serving as Vice-Commander of the Army."[4]

Far more important than Decree-Law 1639 was the one immediately following it. Indeed, one is inevitably tempted to think that Decree-Law 1639 was designed solely to facilitate acceptance of Decree-Law 1640. While the first created a generalship, vice-admiralty or rear-admiralty lacking any real job stability, the second decree-law made the post of commander in chief virtually a lifetime appointment. The precarious position of "general officer in government functions determined by the President of the Republic" contrasted dramatically with the stability of the post of commander in chief, which had no termination date except one that the chiefs themselves might set.

Mandatory retirement of commanders in chief was considered incompatible with the *Statute of the Governing Junta*. Therefore, Decree-Law 1640 dictated that for the four members of the junta, "the grounds for temporary and absolute retirement established by existing legislation have not been nor are they currently applicable, and with respect to said individuals, the only applicable grounds will be those indicated in Article 18 of Decree-Law 527 of 1974."[5] This decree is the *Statute of the Governing Junta*, which established that the commanders in chief of the armed institutions could leave office only due to "death, resignation, or any type of total disability of the incumbent." This statement signified, quite simply, that commanders in chief would hold their appointments for life, unless one of them should decide to step down.

The provision keeping the commanders in chief in office for life will change only when the permanent articles of the Constitution of 1980 take effect. At that time, it will be up to the Chilean President to designate the commanders in chief of the Army, Navy, and Air Force, and the director general of the National Police. There is one important restriction on the selection of new commanders in chief: candidacy will be limited to "the five general officers with most seniority who combine the qualities that the respective institutional statutes require for said positions."[6]

Although the President will designate the commanders in chief, he will not have the power to dismiss them. The Constitution of 1980 is extremely unusual in establishing military posts that are independent of the President of the Republic: "The Commanders in Chief...will serve for four years, may not be nominated for a new term, and may not be removed from their posts."[7]

No democratic regime imaginable would appoint commanders who are independent of political authority and have influence over that authority through a National Security Council where they have the prerogative to publicly express their opinions on "any act, deed, or matter that in their judgment seriously endangers institutional bases or jeopardizes national security."[8] In establishing these procedures the military regime has engineered a sharp contradiction. After rejecting any distinction between the positions of Chief of State and Commander in Chief, it effected a radical reversal by creating a military power that does not have to answer to the President of the Republic. The most elementary political logic leads to the conclusion that a system with these characteristics cannot be maintained because it contains an irreconcilable conflict between the popular will as expressed through the electoral process and the institutional prerogatives of the state's Armed Forces.

Two arguments have been advanced to explain the contradictory power structure created by the Constitution of 1980. The first is that, like other clauses of the document, this section is an *ad nominem* construction. Only a person who for seventeen years has been assembling a corps of generals tailored to his own ambitions and concept of power could govern without fear of an eventual clash with the military that would destroy such an anomalous constitutional order. After the 1989 plebiscite, Pinochet will designate as commander in chief of the Army a general who was seventeen years behind him in military school. This gap implies that when Pinochet was already an army major, his future commander in chief was merely a second lieutenant just out of military school. An even greater age gap will intrude between Pinochet and the youngest generals—some twenty-five years. Further reinforcing Pinochet's total control over the military is the fact that between 1973 and 1989, the careers of these officers will have been determined by the decisions of General Pinochet during his lengthy tenure as Commander in Chief.

A second interpretation of the unusual legal structure of the Constitution of 1980 is that it was designed to establish the incumbency of the present commanders in chief until 1997 or 1998. If General Pinochet is elected in the 1989 plebiscite, the sitting commanders in chief will continue in office because they will not be subject to "the limitation of term stipulated in Article 93 of this Constitution, which will take effect four years after the end of the indicated presidential period" [which began in 1981].

If Pinochet were to lose in 1989 and someone else were elected President in 1990, the new President would not be able to appoint new commanders in chief because according to Article 93 the commanders in chief incumbent at that time are to retain their posts until 1998. This political aberration could result in the election of an opposition President who would inherit the current Governing Junta as commanders in chief for his entire term in office.

The Constitution of 1980 thus institutionalizes a personalized conception of political power and an even greater degree of power over the military structure which Pinochet has used to fortify his control. By 1998 the generals next in seniority to Pinochet will be twenty-six graduating classes behind him, and there will be thirty-four graduating classes between Pinochet and the younger generals.

CHAPTER 13

Controlling Careers

An essential requirement of military professionalism is career stability for officers and promotion by seniority and merit. A corollary that results from this requirement is that in a professional army, decisions affecting nominations, assignments, and retirements must remain free of political interference. In a military dictatorship, however, these criteria are systematically undermined. Because the army is the center of dictatorial political power, personal and political loyalty to the chief of state becomes more important than professional achievement. Political neutrality is suspect, and opinions about matters of state that even slightly contradict the ruler's policies may be punished by early retirement. Consequently, the army becomes political in the worst sense of the word: as an institution, it is required to provide support for executive policies while its officers as individuals are obliged to adhere to those policies.

Chilean historical experience in these matters provides clear and conclusive evidence of this tendency. From 1927 to 1931, the military dictatorship of Colonel Carlos Ibáñez del Campo ruled Chile. As has been shown, the erosion of military professionalism was recognized subsequently by officers of that era, who described the ways in which the mechanisms guaranteeing officers' careers were destroyed.[1] Ibáñez's extensive discretionary powers over the professional lives of his comrades-in-arms bore no relation to the procedures for promotions and career stability that had been established during Chile's many years of democratic rule.

Officers' Careers in the Democratic Regime

In order to analyze the changes in the procedures for promotions and career stability in effect before the 1973 military coup, these procedures must be explained. Guarantees of military career security were originally established by the Constitution of 1925 and subsequent legislation. Promotions and retirements were based on a well-structured system of checks and balances that involved the participation of various authorities as well as collegial military and political bodies. The system established in 1968, and in effect on 11 September 1973, had three stages.[2]

First, unit commanders rated their officers annually, classifying them in one of four categories: those placed on list one were ranked very good, on list two as meritorious, on list three as conditional, and on list four as deficient. Second, the Annual Assessment Boards met to consider these ratings. Each branch of the service had an assessment board composed of general officers (Army division and brigadier generals, Air Force aviation and air brigadier generals, and Naval vice-admirals and rear admirals). Board sessions were presided over by the commander in chief of each branch or by the general following him in seniority. The boards were charged with drafting classification and retirement lists. Retirement lists were ordered as follows: those who had been rated on list four (deficient), those who had been rated for the second time on list three (conditional), those on list three for the first time, those on list two (meritorious), and those on list one (very good).

Those officers on list four and those on list three for the second time were required to leave active service. The number of officers who had to retire was determined before the first meeting of each year's assessment board by the President of the Republic, following the recommendations of the respective commanders in chief. In the third stage, if any officer did not agree with the rating given by the Assessment Board, he had the right to take his case to the Officers' Appeals Board (Junta de Apelación). This board consisted of the minister of defense, the commanders in chief of the Army, Navy, and Air Force, and the general officer next in seniority to the commander in chief of the branch whose rating was under review.

After retirements were decided and the Army list was purged of those required to leave the service, the Assessment Board turned to promotions. This procedure also had three stages. First, officers were promoted in order of seniority. Those on list three (rated conditional) and those accused of military crimes could not be promoted under any circumstances. Certain requirements were necessary for promotion: time in grade, successful completion of courses or examinations concerning regulations, and professional writings. The President of the Republic could "a single time in [an officer's] career," waive "the fulfillment of one or more requirements for promotion, except for that of time in grade."[3] Second, promotions of chief and subordinate officers (all those at or below the ranks of lieutenant colonel, frigate captain, and group commander) were determined by supreme decree, a resolution signed by the President and the minister of defense. Third, nominations of superior officers (Air Force and Army colonels and Navy captains) and generals were made by the President of the Republic, subject to Senate approval.

These were the normal retirement and promotion procedures pertaining to the officer corps. But the President also had certain discretionary powers. First, he could name commanders in chief, who held their posts as long as they retained the President's confidence. If a general who was not highest on the seniority list was named, all those who preceded him on the list would automatically be retired. Second, the President could order the temporary retirement of any officer at any time. An officer in temporary retirement for more than three years was permanently retired. Third, the President could decline to decree the promotion of a chief or subordinate officer or decline to send the document proposing an officer's promotion to the Senate. Finally, the commander in chief had power to effect indirectly the temporary retirement of an officer. Under this procedure, the officer had to remain unassigned for three months or be on call for an equal period of time.

By means of these mechanisms, the Chilean democratic system had established checks and balances to maintain professionalism and career stability in the Armed Forces as well as a system of promotions based on seniority and merit. The participation of various authorities in shaping careers shielded officers from the interference of service factors, political parties, and their military superiors. This system of checks and balances also prevented promotions from depending on the whim of a particular individual or authority. As General Medina Fraguela noted, this system was designed to encourage character, independence, and pride among officers, especially those in the higher ranks.

Under this system, officers' evaluations, and consequently their retirements, were primarily the responsibility of institutional authority. Appeals, however, were taken outside the institution to the Appeals Board, an agency representing the highest professional level of the military. As noted, the appellant's branch of service had a minority of two members on the Appeals Board—the commander in chief of the branch and the officer next in seniority. The other three members of the board were high military officers from other branches. Political representation was limited to one of the five members, the minister of defense.

The composition of the Appeals Board made it possible for an officer who had been evaluated by his own branch of service to take his case to an agency with broader and higher-level representation. The case of Colonel Herman Brady in 1971 illustrates the functioning of this mechanism. Called upon by the Assessment Board to retire, Brady asked the Appeals Board to review his case. Two members of the review voted against him (fellow Army members Generals Prats and Schafauser) while three voted in his favor (Minister of Defense Alejandro Ríos Valdivia and the commanders of the Navy and Air Force, Admiral Montero and General Ruiz Danyau).

Promotions, the other crucial element in a military career, were governed by seniority, which was rigorously established by the Army list and by merit, as evaluated through courses, writings, seminars, and other endeavors. At the highest level, however, promotions were decided upon by the President of the Republic with the concurrence of the Senate, a procedure specified by the constitution for especially important matters.

Before 1973 only the promotion to commander in chief, the most important military rank, was the President's prerogative.

One of the most radical changes in Chile since the September 1973 coup has been the change in the rules governing officers' careers. Yet outside the closed military realm, little or nothing is known about the dramatic changes that undermined the legal protections of military professionalism. These modifications have subverted the checks and balances that previously safeguarded officers' careers, making advancement in the military increasingly subject to the discretion of the military ruler.

But before analyzing these modifications, it will be helpful to draw a brief comparison with another military regime as a means of highlighting the marked traits of the Chilean dictatorship. Many dictatorships have modified or eliminated the regulations designed to guarantee the stability and dignity of officers' careers. In recent South American authoritarian regimes, however, the armed forces have defended themselves against the dictator by using the protection of those laws that affect their status. For example, during the Uruguayan dictatorship of 1973–1985, despite the enormous discretionary power of the regime, the Uruguayan Armed Forces flatly declared that the laws regulating the military system would not be subject to modification. Their stand was facilitated by the power arrangement in Uruguay, in which the posts of president and commander in chief were not held by the same person, and by the fact that the general who occupied the post of commander in chief was subject to the rules governing retirement by seniority. Thus no individual was able to take over as the permanent top military authority.

The Crisis and Officers' Careers

At the time of the military coup in Chile, clear divisions existed within the Armed Forces. Consequently, after the coup, the regime had to devise mechanisms to purge officers who had been committed to the former government or who seemed dangerously disaffected. To that end, the rules governing officers' promotions and retirements in all branches

141

of the Armed Forces were modified substantially. The system that had been in effect during the democratic period was suspended and replaced by one that concentrated unlimited power in the commanders in chief. Provisions were enacted to facilitate the retirement of certain officers. These provisions were perceived by most of the officer corps not as a threat but as a necessity. Immediately after the coup, the Commander in Chief's power was not yet consolidated and the corps of generals was still an important decision-making body that limited Pinochet's discretionary powers. For major decisions, he needed the support of key generals who enjoyed great prestige inside and outside the Army.

On 21 September 1973, just ten days after the coup, the powers of the Officers' Assessment and Appeals Board were suspended. These powers would henceforth be "exercised exclusively by the Commander in Chief of the Army."[4] Control of the entire system of ratings, promotions, and retirements was thus handed over to Pinochet, who had the option to "be advised by the Council of Generals (Consejo de Generales), which will serve as a consultative body only and may convene with 51 percent of the generals in active service."

Three months later, a completely revamped ratings mechanism was implemented that gave the Commander in Chief new powers over promotions and retirements. The decree-law in question (number 220) expressly stated that it was to take effect on the date of its dictation, 24 December 1973, but it was not published in the official government newspaper, the *Diario Oficial*, until ninety days later.[5]

This decree-law introduced profound changes in promotion and retirement procedures, especially for generals, colonels, and their naval counterparts. It also produced a new institution, the Officers' Extraordinary Assessment Board (Junta Calificadora Extraordinaria de Oficiales). As detailed in the decree-law, this new board was empowered to decide certain specific issues and could be convened only by the Commander in Chief of the Army (Pinochet). When one or more generals retired, the Commander in Chief could convene the Extraordinary Board to propose colonels for promotion and retire or place on a complementary list outside the chain

142

of command all those colonels who, "being eligible to be promoted, were not proposed for promotion."

The broad scope of the decree made it possible to use the Extraordinary Boards as a means of taking decisions on colonels' promotions and retirements away from the Assessment Board (that is, the Council of Generals). Ratings—and therefore promotions and retirements—are collective decisions when customary procedure is followed. But under this extraordinary procedure, proposals for promotion to the rank of general have become the exclusive province of the Commander in Chief. The other members of the Assessment Board may only approve or reject such proposals.

The Commander in Chief has even greater power over retirements. Any eligible colonel who is not proposed for promotion by the Commander in Chief must retire or be placed on the complementary list. Even in the hypothetical event that the Commander in Chief's promotions proposal was not accepted, eligible colonels who had not been proposed for promotion by the Commander in Chief would still have to leave active service. It is the absence of a proposal from the Commander in Chief that is the determining factor, regardless of whether an officer with less seniority is promoted over one with more seniority. However one analyzes the mechanism of the Officers' Extraordinary Boards, it is clearly now impossible for a colonel to be promoted to general without the support of the Commander in Chief.

A second occasion that allows for convening the Officers' Extraordinary Board is "when because of special circumstances, authorized by the Commander in Chief, it is necessary to decide on the immediate inclusion of one or more Superior Officers (colonels) or Chiefs (lieutenant colonels or majors) on the extraordinary list of retirements or the complementary list."[6] It should also be noted that decisions of the Extraordinary Assessment Board are final—they may not be appealed.

Despite the importance of the Extraordinary Board, the decree-law that created it did not contain any procedural rules. Regulations concerning majorities required to adopt decisions, formalities for convening the board, or authority to preside over meetings would seem to have been indispensable.

But as the decree was written, it was entirely possible for the board to convene and make decisions with only a minority of the corps of generals in attendance. This deficiency in the legislation was partially corrected seventeen months later, when it was decreed that "the Officers" Extraordinary Assessment Board will be composed of all the General Officers and will be presided over by the division general with the most seniority. In his absence, he will be replaced by the next most senior division general of those present."[7] But nothing was established about such decisive matters as the method of convening, the definition of a quorum, and the majority required for adopting decisions. The most significant aspect of the Extraordinary Board is that although it was created for an emergency situation, it became permanent, being incorporated as part of the general legislation on Armed Forces personnel.[8]

The final legal regulation related to the coup and military career rules dealt with promotion requirements. Before 11 September 1973, a provision in Chilean law had allowed the President to waive the fulfillment of one or more requirements for promotion (except that of time served in grade) a single time in an officer's career. In February 1974, this power was extended to the commanders in chief of the Armed Forces.[10] For sixteen months, from October 1973 through January 1975, the commanders in chief were empowered to waive "the fulfillment of one or more requirements for promotion, except for that of time served in grade."[11] This exemption could be conceded even to someone who had already been so favored by the President of the Republic.

The decree expired 31 January 1975. Ten months later, another decree-law with no termination date reestablished this power. The new decree-law, dated October 1975 and published the following month, was made retroactive to the expiration date of the previous decree. "Therefore," stated the new decree, "resolutions and decrees of waiver and promotion from the date of 1 February 1975 onward may be expedited."[11]

The new decree had one important limitation. It authorized the exemption of personnel "from the fulfillment of one or more requirements for promotion, except for that of time served in grade and that of the assessment."[12] The latter restriction had not been part of the previous decree. But the waiver could be conceded even if the same prerogative had been exercised by the President of the Republic before 11 September 1973 or by the Commander in Chief between October 1973 and January 1975.[13]

All these changes amounted to establishing a kind of permanent state of emergency in terms of military promotions. It made routine a procedure that had been permitted only a single time in an officer's entire career in democratic periods.[14]

What follows is a brief sketch intended to illustrate the degree of instability and discretion that the Military Junta introduced into military careers through successive reforms of the *Statute of the Armed Forces* (*Estatuto de las Fuerzas Armadas*).

Officers' Careers Under the Military Regime: Instability and Discretion

To those unaccustomed to political analysis, it might seem surprising that when the rule of law was destroyed, Chilean Army officers, just like other citizens, lost the prerogatives that had guaranteed career advancement and stability. In fact, the system of checks and balances in the Armed Forces disappeared with the military coup. The authority and powers that the Armed Forces Personnel Statute (Estatuto del Personal de las Fuerzas Armadas) had reserved for the President were combined with those of the Commander in Chief, creating unrestrained power. Further, with the dissolution of the Senate, legislative power was added to the unchecked power of the President–Commander in Chief of the Army.

But the matter did not stop there. By dissolving the Parliament and replacing it with the Military Junta as the legislative authority, the new regime assumed the power to change the laws that had guaranteed the stability of officers' careers and the integrity of the promotions process. These laws, which had remained in force through several administrations, were suddenly at the mercy of a majority decision of the commanders in chief.

In this regard, the Chilean military regime again dif-
fers from its South American counterparts. Other military
governments have tended to zealously maintain regulations
governing the rights and prerogatives of the officer corps.
The practice of changing these provisions as a means of
strengthening the power of the chief of state by increasing
his control over officers' careers has been more characteristic
of *caudillista* ("strong man") or highly personalistic regimes.
Yet these regulations were modified in Chile, a country
previously characterized by a professional military tradition
that was one of the most highly developed—if not *the* most
developed—in Latin America.

Almost a year after the military coup, the entire ratings
system that had existed during the democratic period was
torn out by its roots and replaced by another that had two
basic characteristics: it removed promotions and retirements
from the supervision of any agency outside the corresponding
branch of the Armed Forces; it gave the commanders in
chief much greater power to decide these matters within each branch.[15]

Decree-Law 624 began by changing the name of the
former Assessment Boards to Selection Boards (Juntas de
Selección). This decree-law focused on the Selection Board
of Superior and Chief Officers (majors, lieutenant-colonels,
and colonels), establishing that Army brigadier generals would
be in charge of approving the annual qualifying lists of superior
and chief officers and of making up the list of officers who
would be placed on the complementary list. The board had
power over retirements through the assessment lists because
all officers on list three (rated conditional) for the second
year or on list four (rated deficient) had to retire. The
decree specifically stated that the board had responsibility
for "announcing the list of retirements."

Ranking above the Selection Board of Superior and Chief
Officers is the Officers' Appeals Board, which in the Army was
made up of the commander in chief and the division generals.
The quorum for the Appeals Board was set at a minimum
of three members, with the important qualifier that "if for
overriding reasons the indicated quorum cannot be met, the
brigadier general next in seniority will be named as substitute

voting member." Thus the Appeals Board could function with just two of its seven members and the most senior brigadier general. This small quorum invites comparison with that of the selection boards, which were required by law to have a quorum of "two-thirds the active voting members, even when considering less important issues."[16]

Consistent up to this point was the concept that the brigadier generals are responsible for assessing colonels, lieutenant-colonels, and majors, while division generals, presided over by the commander in chief, are in charge of appeals. This practice represented an attempt to somehow retain the principle that the functions of assessment and appeals should be carried out by different agencies. The Armed Forces Personnel Statute in effect during democratic governments had assigned final resolution of such matters to an appeals board made up of a minority of generals from the branch in question, the minister of defense, and the other commanders in chief.

Decree-Law 624 lasted only a year. In September 1975, important modifications were added to this legislation.[17] The right of brigadier generals to assess superior and chief officers, which had been granted a year earlier, was rescinded. Instead, all general officers (division generals and brigadier generals) would make the assessments.

Although this arrangement was the same one that had existed before the coup, the context had changed. Previously, the division generals had been responsible for assessments, but their decisions were appealed to a different agency. Now the division generals were part of the assessment process at the same time that they participated in the appeals process. Thus the brigadier generals were deprived of any real power in the assessment process, for was it not illusory equality to participate in the adoption of a decision that only some of the participants (the division generals) could reconsider later through appeal?

A new modification strengthening the power of the Commander in Chief was also introduced into the mechanism of the selection boards: "The Recording Secretary for the Boards will be a member officer or the superior officer designated by the Commander in Chief."[18] Thus the vital assignment of minute-taking at secret sessions could be determined by the

Commander in Chief by designating a loyal officer to serve as recording secretary.

Decree-Law 624 of 1974 also reintroduced into Chilean military legislation a mechanism that exacerbated the instability of colonels' careers to a degree that would be difficult to exaggerate. This modification stated that "in the Army, superior officers, on completing thirty years of effective service or three years in grade, will present their letters of resignation. These letters will be considered by the Selection Board and by the Appeals Board of the appropriate year."[19]

This provision has been associated historically with the Ibáñez dictatorship. General Medina Fraguela criticized it in his memoirs for leaving "prestige and perquisites...to the generals" and for diminishing the value of a career in the military. Medina elaborated, "A regulation was enacted requiring the submission of retirement papers starting at the rank of colonel, so that government approval was needed for promotion to general. This measure runs contrary to the highest moral values of a troop leader, those being the character, independence, and pride that comprise a general's personality. With this measure, not only was the leader undercut, but in an indirect way, politics were injected into the Army. It was forgotten that the military serves the interests of the country, regardless of the form of government or the individuals involved in it."[20]

This measure remained in effect after the fall of the Ibáñez dictatorship, as can be inferred from ongoing criticisms that appeared in military publications. Eventually, a democratic government (it was not possible to determine which administration) revoked this unjust and offensive legislation, which does not appear in the Armed Forces Personnel Statute of 1968.

The most striking element of this restored provision is its enormous breadth. The requirement for minimum time in grade for a colonel's promotion to general was four years before 1979 and five years as of Decree-Law 2956 of December 1979. Consequently, all superior officers who desired promotion would have to wait one or two years more before completing the minimum time for promotion.

Another notable element in the provision is the great degree of power over officers' careers, especially at the highest level. By virtue of this legislation, the "request" for retirement of any superior officer, even the most brilliant and accomplished, is subject to approval if he has spent more than three years in grade or more than thirty years in the service. The Assessment Boards have absolute discretion to expedite this retirement.

Perhaps the most aberrant aspect of the provision is its final clause: letters of resignation "that are not accepted will be kept in the Personnel Office as long as the superior officer remains in the service." That is to say, letters of resignation are never rejected—they simply remain pending.

CHAPTER 14

Reshaping the
General Staff

The combination of mechanisms that have been analyzed here, which are the expression of a policy of authoritarian control of the military, have caused profound changes in the Chilean Armed Forces. A full description, however, would go beyond the scope of this work and the self-imposed limitations on sources. Moreover, armies are semisecret institutions that distrust and resist investigation by outsiders. But although these changes are not easily examined from without, it is clear that within the Armed Forces they have been real and deep.

A comparative analysis of the changing composition of the corps of generals illustrates how authoritarian control can alter the Armed Forces (see table 14.1). First, note the corps of generals of 1966, whose commander in chief was General Bernardino Parada. Several observations can be made about these nineteen generals. In all cases, thirty-six years elapsed from the time they were commissioned as officers to the time they became generals. Perhaps more important is the fact that the generals were members of a limited number of military school classes. Commander in Chief Parada was from the class of 1927, all division generals were from the class of 1928, and the fourteen brigade generals had graduated in either 1929 or 1930. The significance of this sequence is that only four years separated the commander in chief from the youngest generals.

Several notable changes are apparent in the corps of generals of August 1973, the last month of Chile's democratic era (see table 14.2). First, the number of generals increased from nineteen to twenty-five in the intervening seven years.

Table 14.1   The Corps of Generals of 1966

Name and Rank	Date of First Commission
General of the Army	
Bernardino Parada	29 December 1927
Division General	
Otto Barth	28 December 1928
Aníbal Mansilla	28 December 1928
Alberto Echaurren	28 December 1928
Hernán Rodríguez	28 December 1928
Brigade General	
Luis Miqueles	24 December 1929
Germán Valdivia	24 December 1929
Juan Bancalari	24 December 1929
Tulio Marambio	24 December 1929
Renzo De Kartzow	24 December 1929
Oscar Guzmán	24 December 1929
Fernando Izurieta	23 December 1930
Jorge Quiroga	23 December 1930
René Cabrera	23 December 1930
Rodolfo Abé	23 December 1930
Sergio Castillo	23 December 1930
Félix Guerrero	23 December 1930
Juan Forch	23 December 1930
Roberto Fuentes	23 December 1930

A concurrent reduction occurred in the time needed to rise to the rank of general. Washington Carrasco, the most junior of the twenty-five, was commissioned as an officer in 1942 and attained the rank of general thirty-one years later.

Second, the 1973 corps of generals encompassed a broader range of military school graduating classes. Commander in Chief Prats graduated in 1934. None of the 1973 corps came from the classes of 1935 or 1936. The six division generals came from the classes of 1937, 1938, and 1939, and the eighteen brigade generals graduated between 1939 and 1942. The distance between the Commander in Chief Prats and the youngest general was thus nine years. In comparison with the

Table 14.2 The Corps of Generals of 1973

Name and Rank	Date of First Commission
General of the Army	
Carlos Prats	1 January 1934
Division General	
Augusto Pinochet	1 January 1937
Orlando Urbina	1 January 1937
Rolando González	1 January 1938
Manuel Torres	1 January 1938
Ernesto Baeza	1 January 1939
Oscar Bonilla	1 January 1939
Brigade General	
Ervaldo Rodríguez	1 January 1939
Ricardo Valenzuela	1 January 1939
Héctor Bravo	1 January 1939
Mario Sepúlveda	1 January 1939
Guillermo Pickering	1 January 1939
Herman Brady	1 January 1939
Pedro Palacios	1 January 1939
Raúl Contreras	1 January 1940
Raúl Benavides	1 January 1940
Joaquín Lagos	1 January 1940
Gustavo Alvarez	1 January 1940
Carlos Forestier	1 January 1940
Arturo Viveros	1 January 1940
Sergio Nuño	1 January 1941
Sergio Arellano	1 January 1941
Augusto Lutz	1 January 1942
Javier Palacios	1 January 1942
Washington Carrasco	1 January 1942

four years that separated the 1966 group. The explanation for this situation lies in the enormous difficulties experienced by the military in 1932 and the years following. After the fall of the Ibáñez dictatorship, a strong antimilitary reaction plunged the profession to its lowest level of public prestige. This steep decline was reflected in the reduced number and poor quality of those who chose to pursue military careers.

Seven years after the military coup, the corps of generals displayed the characteristics illustrated on table 14.3. The corps of generals had expanded from twenty-five members in 1973 to thirty-nine members by 1980. This increase is only partially explained by Decree-Law 1639 of 1976, which altered seniority retirement rules. Each time the decree-law excepted a general from retirement, "the number of generals would be temporarily increased in the respective institutions."[1] The time required to attain the rank of general, measured from the date of nomination of the most junior officer, also decreased, in this case to twenty-nine years. A further change was the establishment of the rank of lieutenant general, a fourth category of general that falls between the ranks of general of the army and division general. Analysis of the 1980 corps of generals shows that the most important effect of this new rank has been to increase the distance separating the Commander in Chief from the division generals in the pyramid of the military hierarchy. As noted in the previous chapter, lieutenant generals receive discretionary assignments that usually fall outside the institutional line of command.

The age gap between the commander in chief and the rest of the generals, measured in number of graduating classes, became an abyss. Six graduating classes intervened between Pinochet and the vice-commander in chief, the next general in the line of command. At the other end, the youngest general, Sergio Badiola, became an officer fourteen years after General Pinochet; that is to say, when Badiola was finishing military school, Pinochet was already a major on the verge of becoming a lieutenant colonel or commander.

Between 1978 and 1981, an attempt was made to reverse the shortened duration of officers' careers. By 1979 changes in the military profession during the authoritarian period had greatly reduced the length of time an officer spent in active service. In an effort to reverse this trend, the military high command established the new rank of third lieutenant (alférez). The minimum requirements for time in grade for officers were also extended, as is illustrated in table 14.4.[2]

But the reform that most directly affected the corps of generals was the renaming of officers' ranks. The corps of

Table 14.3   The Corps of Generals of 1980

Name and Rank	Date of First Commission	
General of the Army		
Augusto Pinochet	1 January	1937
Lieutenant General		
Herman Brady	1 January	1939
Raúl Benavides	1 January	1940
Division General		
Washington Carrasco	1 January	1942
Augustín Toro	1 January	1942
Nilo Floody	1 January	1942
Rolando Garay	1 January	1942
Julio Canessa	1 January	1944
Sergio Covarrubias	1 January	1944
Joaquín Ramírez	23 December	1944
Enrique Morel	23 December	1944
Brigade General		
Sixto Rubio	23 December	1944
Carol Urzúa	23 December	1944
Rafael Ortiz	1 January	1946
Patricio Torres	1 January	1946
Héctor Orozco	1 January	1946
Humberto Gordon	1 January	1947
Carlos Morales	1 January	1947
Guillermo Toro	1 January	1947
Luis Prussing	1 January	1947
Osvaldo Hernández	1 January	1947
Enrique Valdés	1 January	1948
Santiago Sinclair	1 January	1948
Julio Fernández	1 January	1948
Cristián Ackernecht	1 January	1948
René Vidal	1 January	1948
Dante Iturriaga	1 January	1949
Carol Lopicich	1 January	1949
Luis Danús	1 January	1949
Julio Jara	1 January	1949
Iván Dobud	1 January	1949
Alejandro Medina	1 January	1950

Table 14.3 The Corps of Generals of 1980
(continued)

Name and Rank	Date of First Commission	
Brigade General		
Manuel Barros	1 January	1949
Jorgee O'Ryan	1 January	1950
Rolando Figueroa	1 January	1949
Jorge Dowling	1 January	1950
Roberto Soto	1 January	1951
José Mutis	1 January	1951
Sergio Badiola	1 January	1951

Table 14.4 Changes in Requirements for
Time to Achieve Rank

Rank	Required before 1979 (years)	Required since 1979 (years)
Second Lieutenant	–	1
Sublieutenant	3	3
Lieutenant	4	5
Captain	5	6
Major	5	5
Lieutenant Colonel	5	5
Colonel	4	5
Brigade General	2	2

generals was subdivided into ranks whose titles broke with the past. This process began with the creation of the rank of lieutenant general. Commander in Chief Pinochet told the highest military circle:

Gentlemen, you may have noticed this denomination of lieutenant general, in use for the first time in Chile. The rank of general is a modern one, for as you will remember

Gonzalo de Córdoba was called Gran Capitán because he coordinated the captains. Then the rank of general appeared, beginning in the sixteenth century. The term "lieutenant general" comes from "lugarteniente," the one who was second to the general.... I also remind you that our rank of general came into being on 31 July 1837. Since then we have had the ranks of division general and brigade general, which replaced the corresponding Spanish ranks of brigadier and field marshall.[3]

An additional change in the denomination of generals' ranks was made in June 1981. The title "captain general" was given to the officer who occupied the post of commander in chief of the Army, and the title of "Generalissimo" was bestowed on the person serving as President of the Republic. The law also established a transitory disposition authorizing "the titular Commander in Chief of the Army on the date of publication of this law" to retain the title of "General of the Army." Thus Pinochet simultaneously became General of the Army (or Captain General) and Generalissimo of the Armed Forces.

The rank of lieutenant general was retained as the second-highest in the Army. The rank of division general was changed to major general, and that of brigade general to brigadier general. Colonels would become "brigadiers" after four years in grade. The denomination of "brigadier" would not constitute a grade; neither would it affect requirements of time in grade nor entail higher pay.

After these changes, the Chilean Army ranks consisted of ten levels: third lieutenant, second lieutenant, lieutenant, captain, major, lieutenant colonel or commander, colonel, brigadier, brigadier general, major general, lieutenant general, and captain general. The official reasons for these changes are obscure. One Army spokesperson justified them by saying that "the goal of enacting the publically disclosed modifications is to reconcile Army officers' ranks with similar ranks in the armed forces of other countries. It has been noted, for example, that the armies of Argentina, Uruguay, Spain, and other countries have such ranks in their respective echelons."[4] Regardless of the intention, these changes ended one of the oldest traditions of the Chilean Army, the ranks of division and brigade general, which dated from 1837.

In 1984, eleven years after the installation of the authoritarian regime, the general corps looked as is shown in table 14.5. This list does not include the generals in charge of the departments of health, justice, and the Deputy War General (Vicario General Castrense).

The nature, structure, and ranks of this corps of generals differ radically from all previous ones. The tendency to expand the number of generals continued, creating a notable trend: from nineteen generals in 1966, the number climbed to twenty-five in 1973, forty in 1980, and fifty-one in 1984. Meanwhile, the time required for the officer with the least seniority to attain the rank of general fell to twenty-eight years by 1984, despite the effort of the decree-law in 1979 to reverse this tendency. Two years later, in 1986, the corps of generals assumed the composition shown in table 14.6.

The Chilean corps of generals is assembled and its members are assigned duties by a particular procedure. Each year, the Assessment Board of Superior Officers and Army Chiefs, presided over by Captain General Augusto Pinochet, submits to the Commander in Chief (again, Pinochet) the names of those whom the board proposes to promote to brigadier general. Official Army communiqués demonstrate transparently this extreme concentration of military power. For example, in 1984 the government-owned newspaper, *La Nación*, reported: "The second phase of the Assessment Board of Superior Officers and Army Chiefs, presided over by His Excellency the President of the Republic, Captain General Augusto Pinochet Ugarte, finished at midday yesterday. At the end of this session, the Commander in Chief resolved the following: to approve the propositions for promotion to the rank of brigadier general presented by the officers' assessment board."[5]

Through this procedure, the Commander in Chief alone, unburdened by the obligation to consult any governmental or military agency, is empowered to make four major categories of decisions. First, he can accept the resignations of the generals who are eligible for retirement. "In terms of those general officers who seek to retire, His Excellency the President of the

Table 14.5   The Corps of Generals of 1984

Name and Rank	Date of First Commission
General of the Army or Captain General	
Augusto Pinochet	1 January 1937
Lieutenant General	
Raúl Benavides	1 January 1940
Julio Canessa	1 January 1944
Major General	
Humberto Gordon	1 January 1947
Luis Prussing	1 January 1947
Osvaldo Hernández	1 January 1947
Enrique Valdés	1 January 1948
Santiago Sinclair	1 January 1948
Cristián Ackernecht	1 January 1948
René Vidal	1 January 1948
Brigadier General	
Luis Danús	1 January 1949
Alejandro Medina	1 January 1950
Manuel Barros	1 January 1950
Jorge O'Ryan	1 January 1950
Jorge Dowling	1 January 1950
Roberto Soto	1 January 1951
Sergio Badiola	1 January 1951
Gabriel Pizarro	1 January 1951
Roberto Guillard	1 January 1951
Alfredo Calderón	1 January 1951
Julio Bravo	1 January 1951
Claudio López	1 January 1951
Gastón Frez	1 January 1952
Arturo Alvarez	1 January 1952
Belarmino López	1 January 1952
Eduardo Ibáñez	1 January 1952
César Manríquez	1 January 1952
Bruno Siebert	1 January 1953
Washington García	1 January 1953
Carlos Meirelles	1 January 1953
Sergio Pérez	1 January 1953

Table 14.5 The Corps of Generals of 1984 (continued)

Name and Rank	Date of First Commission
Brigade General	
Gustavo Rivera	1 January 1953
Luis Reyes	1 January 1954
Julio Salazar	1 January 1954
Carlos Ojeda	1 January 1954
Manuel Matas	1 January 1954
Jorge Zincke	1 January 1955
Jaime González	1 January 1955
Mario Navarrete	1 January 1955
Samuel Rojas	1 January 1955
Francisco Martínez	1 January 1955
Helmut Kraushaar	1 January 1955
Fernando Hormazabal	1 January 1955
Eduardo Castellón	1 January 1955
Julio Andrade	1 January 1955
Sergio Valenzuela	1 January 1955
Aureliano Tello	1 January 1955
Jorge Lucar	1 January 1956
Patricio Gualda	1 January 1956
Hugo Salas	1 January 1956
Hugo Prado	1 January 1956

Republic accepted the following retirements.... "[6] Second, he can decide which generals may continue in the Army, regardless of the obligation to retire on the basis of seniority, because "they are carrying out government functions, as determined by the President of the Republic through supreme decree." Third, he can decide which brigadier generals will be promoted to the rank of major general. In this case, there is one significant limitation on Pinochet's power: he must respect the order of seniority. But he may determine freely how many brigadier generals will be promoted. Finally, once the corps of generals is constituted, the Commander in Chief can appoint the generals he wishes to posts in the Army high command and in the government. Consequently, the same list contains the names of those appointed as chiefs of

Table 14.6   The Corps of Generals of 1986

Name and Rank	Date of First Commission
General of the Army or Captain General	
Augusto Pinochet	1 January 1937
Lieutenant General	
Humberto Gordon	1 January 1947
Santiago Sinclair	1 January 1948
Major General	
Manuel Barros	1 January 1950
Jorge O'Ryan	1 January 1950
Roberto Soto	1 January 1951
Sergio Badiola	1 January 1951
Roberto Guillard	1 January 1951
Alfredo Calderón	1 January 1951
Julio Bravo	1 January 1951
Claudio López	1 January 1951
Brigadier General	
Arturo Alvarez	1 January 1952
Belarmino López	1 January 1952
Eduardo Ibáñez	1 January 1952
Bruno Siebert	1 January 1953
Washington García	1 January 1953
Carlos Ojeda	1 January 1954
Manuel Matas	1 January 1954
Jorge Zincke	1 January 1955
Jaime González	1 January 1955
Mario Navarrete	1 January 1955
Samuel Rojas	1 January 1955
Francisco Martínez	1 January 1955
Helmut Kraushaar	1 January 1955
Fernando Hormazabal	1 January 1955
Eduardo Castellón	1 January 1955
Julio Andrade	1 January 1955
Sergio Valenzuela	1 January 1955
Aureliano Tello	1 January 1955
Jorge Lucar	1 January 1956
Patricio Gualda	1 January 1956

Table 14.6 The Corps of Generals of 1986
(continued)

Name and Rank	Date of First Commission
Brigadier General	
Hugo Salas	1 January 1956
Hugo Prado	1 January 1956
Luis Serre	1 January 1956
Francisco Ramírez	1 January 1956
Hernán Chacón	1 January 1956
Luis Henríquez	1 January 1956
Rodrigo Sánchez	1 January 1956
Renato Fuenzalida	1 January 1956
Mario Varela	1 January 1956
Jaime Núñez	1 January 1957
Jorge Ballerino	1 January 1957
Raúl Iturriaga	1 January 1957
Ernesto Videla	1 January 1957
Hernán Saldes	1 January 1957
Enrique López	1 January 1957
Alejandro González	1 January 1957
Miguel Espinoza	1 January 1957
Héctor Darrigrandi	1 January 1958
Carlos Parera	1 January 1958

staff, military division and brigade commanders, rectors of major universities, ministers of state, military attachés, the director of the Centro Nacional de Informaciones (CNI), and members of the Military Junta.

This extreme concentration of power has opened the door to highly arbitrary management of the Army, as was illustrated by events within the highest military circle between 1984 and 1986. In late 1986, CNI Director General Humberto Gordon was promoted to the post of junta member, Chile's highest political or military post after those occupied by Pinochet. An infantry officer like Pinochet, Gordon had been named general director of the CNI (the secret police) in July 1980. In October 1984, however, the country was startled by the news that Gordon (by then a major general) had retired. A communiqué from the government information office published in Santiago's major newspapers said, "His Excellency the President of the Republic accepted the retirements of Major General Humberto Gordon."[7] But the notice went on to say that "the Commander in Chief of the Army has designated to the posts of institutional high command and government the following general officers," among them Humberto Gordon, who was to continue as director of the CNI.

Major General Gordon was due to retire, but because he was performing "government functions as determined by the President of the Republic," the provisions of Decree-Law 1639 of 1976 applied to him, and he could continue in active service outside the chain of command. Generals Luis Prussing and Osvaldo Hernández were in the same position, the latter being named Intendant of Santiago.

The reasons why Gordon was retained on active duty became clearer when the composition of the 1985 corps of generals was made public. In November of that year, the retirement of Major General Prussing made Gordon and Hernández the only remaining officers of the 1947 military school class. Both were serving in government posts. All of the major generals from the military class of 1948 (Enrique Valdés, Cristián Ackernecht, and René Vidal) retired in 1985, with the exception of Santiago Sinclair. Sinclair was named vice-commander in chief of the Army and was later promoted to lieutenant general. With these changes, the highest circles of the Army began to develop a structure that surprised observers of the rigid Chilean military hierarchy (see table 14.7). The anomaly was that Sinclair now outranked Gordon, although he had graduated a year after Gordon. This unusual circumstance was rationalized on the grounds that Gordon—like Hernández—remained in the Army only while serving as CNI director. But the situation still caused confusion because after the Army announced Gordon's retirement in 1984, it announced in 1985 that he would stay in the service. In any case, it was clear that Sinclair held the higher rank, and that he (not Gordon) was the general who followed Pinochet in seniority.

Table 14.7 Upper Ranks of the Corps
of Generals in 1985

Name and Rank	Date of First Commission
General of the Army or Captain General	
Augusto Pinochet	1 January 1937
Lieutenant General	
Julio Canessa	1 January 1944
Santiago Sinclair	1 January 1948
Major General	
Humberto Gordon	1 January 1947

The surprises of that three-year period in Gordon's career did not end there. The announcement of new promotions, retirements, and assignments in late 1986 brought Gordon two pieces of news, one of them unusual. The first was his promotion to lieutenant general, which made him fourth in seniority after Pinochet, Canessa, and Sinclair. The second was his appointment to the Military Junta, replacing Canessa. This choice conflicted with the constitution, which stated in Transitional Article 14 that Pinochet "will not be a member of the Military Junta and in his place, as titular member, will be the General of the Army who follows him in seniority." With Canessa retiring, Gordon was third, not second, in seniority.

Given these circumstances, Gordon could not be named to the Military Junta unless a special law were dictated that not only named him lieutenant general but awarded him more seniority than Lieutenant General Sinclair, who had been named lieutenant general the year before. That is precisely what happened when what was immediately dubbed the "Gordon law" was published on 2 October. This law overrode several rules of the Armed Forces Personnel Statute.[8] Five days later, Gordon, the new lieutenant general, was named as Pinochet's representative to the Military Junta.

But the irregularities did not begin or end with Gordon. Pinochet's discretion over promotions is further illustrated by the case of Luis Serre, who was promoted after other officers of the graduating class following his, and Mario Varela, who was not promoted with the members of his military class in 1984, nor in 1985, but rather two years late.

The following analysis will consider several characteristics of the corps of generals; the number of generals in each grade, the kind of assignments that correspond to each grade, and the stability of these assignments.

The number of members occupying each grade of general has varied over the years. The number of lieutenant generals remained constant at two in 1980, 1984, and 1986. The number of major generals has increased slightly in comparison with the number of division generals (as they were formerly called) in previous corps of generals: six division generals in 1973, eight in 1980, seven major generals in 1984, ten in 1985, and eight in 1986.

It should be kept in mind that three of the seven major generals serving in 1984—Gordon, Prussing, and Hernández——remained on active duty only because they were occupying government posts at Pinochet's discretion. Therefore, their military status was by definition precarious. While serving in government posts, all three were relieved of military command. By 1985 only two major generals, Gordon and Hernández, remained in that position, and by 1986, there were none.

The slight increase in the number of major generals (formerly called division generals) contrasts sharply with the great increase in the number of brigadier generals. The "inflation" in the total number of generals is clearly concentrated in the grade of brigadier general. There were eighteen brigadier generals in 1973, twenty-eight in 1980, and forty in 1984 and 1986. This dramatic increase in the number of brigadier generals must surely have a negative effect on the prestige and influence associated with this rank.

It is instructive to examine the kinds of duties that the Commander in Chief assigns to each grade. Lieutenant generals are the only generals with specific functions. The lieutenant general with the most seniority is one of the four members of the Military Junta, while the second-ranking lieutenant general is vice-commander in chief. Pinochet enjoys great discretion over the assignments of major generals and brigadier generals. The controlling principle seems to be that no position is protected. All generals must be available for various duties, and neither grade nor seniority guarantees any assignment.

When Major General Sinclair was promoted to second in seniority in the Army, his job as Minister Secretary General of Government (Ministro Secretario General del Gobierno) was taken over by a brigadier general who was thirty-seventh in seniority. When Humberto Gordon took over as Army representative on the Military Junta, he was replaced by General Hugo Salas, thirty-third in seniority. The commander of the Santiago garrison in 1984 was Major General René Vidal, tenth in seniority in the Army. The following year the commander was Brigadier General Carlos Ojeda, twenty-sixth in seniority, and in 1986, it was Brigadier General Jorge Zincke, twentieth in seniority.

While some officers relatively low in the hierarchy were assigned to the highest posts, others near the top of the hierarchy were given second-level military duties, as is exemplified by the case of Major General Luis Danús. In 1985 Danús was the most senior general who was not past due for retirement, ranking sixth in seniority. Nevertheless, he was assigned to none of the posts that had traditionally corresponded to his rank: chief of the General Staff, inspector general of the Army, or commander of the Santiago garrison.

The ruling principle of Pinochet's military politics seems to be that no one will be allowed to become established in any position. The status of the lieutenant generals demonstrates that even the post of Army representative to the Military Junta has become an increasingly insecure position. Pinochet held that post for seven and a half years. Raúl Benavides, Pinochet's chosen successor, stayed in the post from March 1981 to December 1985, four and a half years. Canessa, who replaced Benavides, held the post just one year, from December 1985 until December 1986, when he was replaced by Humberto Gordon. Table 14.8 lists several important

Table 14.8 Rotation of Commanders
in Key Military Posts

Post	1984	1985	1986
Chief of Staff	Valdés	O'Ryan	O'Ryan
Inspector General	Ackernecht	Barros	Barros
Commander Santiago Garrison	Vidal	Ojeda	Zincke
Commander Division I	Calderón	Meirelles	Sánchez
Commander Division II	Rojas	Rojas	Núñez
Commander Division III	Ibáñez	Ibáñez	Ibáñez
Commander Division IV	Castellón	Castellón	Iturriaga
Commander Division V	Toro	González	González
Commander Division VI	Dowling	Frez	García
Commander Division VII	González	Sánchez	Saldes

military positions and their incumbents between 1984 and 1986. Included are division commanders and the commander of the Seventh Brigade, who have tended to be removed from positions of troop command.

Only one of the ten military commands analyzed here (the Third Division) has been led by the same officer for three years. Five posts have been occupied by two individuals, and four posts have been occupied by a different commander in each of the three years. It should be added that the position of division commander in chief suffers from an intrinsic military weakness. With the exception of the Second Division (which is based in Santiago), each division commander also serves as the intendant of the capital city of his region, which makes him the highest official in the local government. The commander of the First Division is the intendant of Antofagasta, while the commander of Third Division is the intendant of Concepción. Similar arrangements are found in Valdivia (Fourth Division), Punta Arenas (Fifth Division), Iquique (Sixth Division), and Aysén (Seventh Brigade). This dual assignment led Pinochet to create the post of division vice-commander in chief, to which he assigns a low-seniority brigadier general. The vice-commander becomes the de facto military commander, while his superior is occupied with governing the region. Here the classic maxim of "divide and conquer" has found a new application.

The same principle of dividing all power that does not belong to Pinochet can also be seen in the division of the corps of generals into two distinct hierarchies, one political and the other military, and in the continuous shuffling of the generals from one to the other. By these means, Pinochet prevents any one person from accumulating a significant amount of power, either in the Army or in government. Two separate chains of command and influence exist. The military chain of command is headed by Pinochet as Captain General, followed by the vice-commander in chief and the military post commanders, including the division vice-commanders. The political chain of command is also headed by Pinochet as Captain General, followed by Pinochet's representative to the Military Junta and then the generals holding political posts: intendants, ministers (Bruno Siebert in Public Works and Sergio Valenzuela in the General Secretariat of the Presidency), university rectors (Roberto Soto at the University of Chile and Patricio Gualda at the University of Santiago), the officer for legislative functions (Alejandro González), the officer for Police (Hugo Salas), and administrators (Fernando Hormazalab, vice-president of CORFO, and Hugo Prado, director of Sports and Recreation).

The gap in terms of graduating classes between the Commander in Chief of the Army and the other generals continues to grow. Ten years elapsed between Pinochet's class and that of the highest major general in 1984; by 1986 the distance was thirteen years. The most junior member of the corps of generals in 1984 was Brigadier General Hugo Prado, who was commissioned twenty years after Pinochet. In 1986 the most junior member was Carlos Parera, who graduated twenty-two military classes after Captain General Pinochet. In a staff displaying such great differences of age, any esprit de corps or sense of equality has completely disappeared. Pinochet can rest assured that he heads a group of generals who not only owe him their promotions but relate to him as lieutenants relate to their general.

In his memoirs, General Carlos Prats has described the "overall evolution of the Chilean military sector." He distinguishes five generations of officers during the period of the Frei presidency (1964–1970).[9]

First came the generals who entered military school between 1929 and 1932 and experienced at the beginning of their careers "the bitter vicissitudes of the civilian antimilitary reaction" that followed the fall of Ibáñez in 1931. The last of these generals was Prats himself, who was commissioned in January 1934.

The second generation corresponded to the graduating classes of 1933 through 1938. In this period after the dictatorship, a career in the military was not highly regarded socially, and the few who attended military school were educated under poor institutional conditions. The only general remaining in the service from that period is Pinochet.

The third generation consists of those officers who entered military school during World War II and the Cold War, between 1939 and 1948. Prats observes that they "were characterized by their unconcealable sympathy with the Nazi cause." The last active members of this group are now leaving the service, having completed thirty-eight years as officers. They include current Major Generals Valdés, Sinclair, Ackernecht, and Vidal, who were commissioned in 1948.

A fourth generation is made up of those who attended military school between 1949 and 1957, the last cadets educated in the "old fortress" on Blanco Encalada Street. Prats describes them as having a "decidedly anticommunist mentality." These officers now make up the entire corps of generals. Their most senior members were promoted to the rank of major general in 1986, and the youngest are the most junior brigadier generals.

The fifth generation, which began in 1958, was trained at the new military school. Prats defines this generation as "educated in the counterinsurgency concept derived from [the idea of] 'peaceful coexistence.' Their military training was diversified by the introduction of commando, parachute, and antiguerrilla instruction. Large contingents of young officers attended short courses at the [U.S. Army] School of the Americas, which gave these groups a definite pro-United

States orientation."[10] If the time span of this generation is extended to 1967, when the military events comprising the background of this book began, the graduating classes of those years include all of the current colonels, lieutenant colonels, and commanders.

Prats did not attempt to describe the later graduating classes. Interested readers can find the elements for defining the characteristics of the graduating classes now in the ranks of major and below in the peculiar characteristics of the promotions described in this book. Clearly, the changes that have been wrought in the Chilean Armed Forces are likely to be significant, given the remarkable longevity of the regime that we have been considering.

Epilogue

Where is
Chile Heading?

The standoff in Chilean politics remained as curious and troubling in late 1987 as it was during the previous two years. The situation can best be described by the terms *stalemate* and *catastrophic balance*. In chess, a stalemate occurs when one player can keep the opposing king under constant threat but cannot checkmate him and win the game. In such a situation, the game is declared a draw. *Catastrophic balance* is a term that political scientists apply to a situation in which two opposing social forces have become approximately equal in power, with the result being neither can impose conditions on the other. At the same time, neither will negotiate or compromise. This balance has a catastrophic effect on the society and ends up destroying social cooperation and the political system.

The current political deadlock is due in part to the completely separate bases of support of the two opposing forces in Chile. General Pinochet's power rests almost entirely on the state apparatus, and more specifically on the Chilean military. The extraordinary concentration of authority in the executive branch and the military's domination of domestic and international affairs are General Pinochet's sources of power. As Commander in Chief of the Armed Forces, Pinochet exercises complete institutional and personal control over a united, obedient, hierarchical, and nondeliberative military whose structure has been reshaped since 1973 by what has been characterized as "distorted professionalism."

In Pinochet's regime, power struggles between the executive and the legislative branches of government are virtually nonexistent. The dominance of the executive branch is

facilitated by the existence of a Military Junta that functions only as a second-rank political power. Nor are there
serious conflicts with the judicial branch, which has meekly
submitted to the will of the executive with few exceptions
and has proven itself incapable of protecting the lives and
safety of the citizens.

Although the Pinochet government has received significant support from various civilian groups, it is perhaps the
most thoroughly militarized regime in the history of South
American authoritarian governments. One study of military
participation in Pinochet's government showed that almost
half of the 118 cabinet ministers between 1973 and 1986 were
members of the Armed Forces.[1] Further, the legislative organ
of the dictatorship, which is made up of four commissions, has
been markedly military. From March 1981 to August 1986,
fifty-one members of those commissions (46 percent) came
from the armed services.

Analysis of the governmental structure at the local level also
indicates a high degree of militarization. Chile is divided into
thirteen regions, which are subdivided into fifty provinces.
In each region, the highest authority is the intendant, and
in each province, the governor. In August 1986, all thirteen
intendants were military officers on active duty, as were
forty-two of the fifty governors.

The military takeover of the universities has been one
of the most extreme manifestations of militarization. From
the period immediately following the coup through August
1986, only 13 percent of the rectors of Chile's eight most
important universities were academics. Sixty-four percent of
the rectors were retired military officers, and 23 percent were
officers on active duty.

The militarization of the foreign service has been equally
extreme. Forty-five percent of the personnel directing Chilean
embassies between 1973 and August 1986 were members of the
military. In August 1986, thirteen years after the dictatorship
took power, 33 percent of the heads of diplomatic missions
were members of the Armed Forces.

Another target of military penetration has been state enterprises. Thirty-eight percent of the directors of state enterprises
in June 1986 were members of the Armed Forces. Similarly,

fifteen of the eighteen presidents of state enterprises under CORFO, the Chilean development agency, were military personnel.

Faced with this all-powerful and highly militarized state, one might conclude that if any political opposition has existed, it must be totally ineffectual. Certainly, the Chilean opposition has failed in the sense that until now, and after fifteen years of a struggle that has attracted world attention, it has not been able to overthrow the Pinochet regime. But considered from a different perspective, the opposition has from the outset achieved remarkable success. This opposition in the broadest sense includes not only political parties but intellectual and artistic circles; the independent media, especially radio and magazines; the movements of workers, professionals, and students; and moral forces such as the Catholic Church and the extensive network of lawyers defending human rights.

Operating from social, political, and international bases, this multifaceted opposition has salvaged the fundamental elements of Chile's social and political structure. It has rescued and taken control of what is often called civil society—the thousands of nongovernment organizations used by citizens to further ethical and ideological objectives, to represent and defend economic and social interests, and to undertake political projects. In these realms, the power of the opposition has been affirmed in several ways.

Chile now has a vigorous, well-organized system of political parties. Particularly strong are the Christian Democratic party, the Communist party, and (despite internal divisions) the Socialist party. Moreover, although the process has inevitably entered periods of advance and retreat, the democratic political parties have achieved an ever-widening consensus, as has been detailed in the first part of this book. This growing consensus was expressed first in the Democratic Alliance and then in the National Accord for Full Transition to Democracy.

The democratic political parties also control most of the professional associations, trade unions and labor confederations, although the power of the last two is constantly undermined by the threat of unemployment. Augmenting the political parties is a powerful student movement, which has proven its ability to agitate effectively, as well as the active political movement in the *poblaciones.*

Perhaps one of the strongest elements of the democratic opposition is a factor external to it—the Catholic Church. The Church uses its power and influence to defend human rights, seek changes in the constitution, and support such acts as the National Accord for Full Transition to Democracy. The most influential bishops have committed themselves to support the demand for free elections.

Finally, the Chilean opposition draws much of its strength from highly sympathetic international public opinion and the backing of most of the governments of Europe and the Americas. This worldwide support for the Chilean opposition contrasts sharply with the international isolation of the Pinochet regime.

What distinguishes recent Chilean politics is the stalemated aspect of the clash between the government and the opposition. The two forces apparently have achieved equivalent degrees of political power, although this power derives from sources that are unequal in nature. The government has developed a powerful state structure based on the military as its source of power. The opposition, in contrast, controls civil society, where Pinochet's limited influence derives almost exclusively from state clientelism.

General Pinochet has remained strong enough to stay in power but not strong enough to destroy the opposition. For its part, the opposition has maintained its overwhelming influence in student, worker, professional, *población,* and party organizations, despite the states of siege and other forms of government pressure. Yet the opposition is not strong enough to bring down the dictatorship. Since the early 1980s, this catastrophic balance of power has resulted in a political war of attrition with no apparent solution.

But where is the conflict leading? What are the possibilities that in the near future one of these contending forces will emerge victorious from this conflict? Pinochet's response to this stalemate can be found in the constitution that was pushed through in 1980.[2] According to this document, at least ninety days before 11 March 1989 (the date when

Pinochet is to step down from the presidency), it will be up to the commanders in chief and the general director of the National Police to "propose to the country, by unanimous agreement,...subject to ratification by the citizenry, the person who will occupy the post of President of the Republic" for the following eight years. Because this person will not be subject to the "prohibition against being re-elected," the way is open for Pinochet's candidacy. If the commanders in chief and the director general of the National Police fail to agree unanimously, the nomination will be made by "the National Security Council, by the majority of its members," an organization in which Pinochet has three votes at the outset (his own and those of two loyal functionaries). The nominee will then be submitted to a yes-or-no vote in a plebiscite.

The significance of this electoral process is that after fifteen and a half years of Pinochet's regime, the opposition will not have the option to present an alternate presidential candidate to the one proposed by the military government. Technically, then, this presidential election cannot be considered a "free election." It would not be free even if the state of emergency were revoked during the period preceding the election and if access to communications media were equitable. The essence of a free election is that the opposition can present an alternate candidate of its own.

The Constitution of 1980 stipulates that if the regime's candidate is defeated in the plebiscite, a competitive election for President and members of Parliament will be scheduled for the following year. In the event that the opposition wins that election—that is, defeats the regime for a second time—the Constitution of 1980 provides for the creation of a military power independent of the elected civilian government. It also stipulates that the individuals serving as commanders in chief and director general of the National Police at the end of the transition period are to remain in their posts until 1997. These could easily be the current commanders in chief: Augusto Pinochet, José Toribio Merino, Fernando Matthei, and Rodolfo Stange. In this way, the President elected in 1990 will be deprived of control of the military throughout his term in office, even if he is the bitterest foe of the Pinochet regime. Consequently, regardless of who is elected, during the first government after the dictatorship, military power will be retained by the commanders in chief of the military regime.

In response to this strategy of Pinochet's and in order to tilt the "catastrophic balance" in its own favor, the democratic opposition has developed a surprising policy based on the electoral process stipulated in the Constitution of 1980. Several factors led to this strategy. One is the mere passage of time and the inevitability of the 1989 plebiscite mandated by the Constitution of 1980. Additional circumstances include the failure to achieve the constitutional reform proposed by the National Accord for Full Transition to Democracy, the failure to sustain a "national strike" in the terms presented by the Civil Assembly, and the setback suffered by the opposition as a whole following the discovery of the Communist party's arsenals and the 1986 attempt on Pinochet's life. Given these conditions, the democratic opposition accepted the electoral confrontation established by the Constitution of 1980 as the most likely outcome of the conflict.

Certainly, the decision to observe the electoral guidelines of a constitution such as Pinochet's, which was created to perpetuate dictatorship and impede democracy, is not without risks. From the outset, the danger arises of being trapped in its mechanisms. But how much difference can a constitution make when faced with the enormous and complex reality of politics? The question is germane because no historical process can be reduced to a constitutional document. Constitutions and laws are only the formal element of the political process.

In societies where basic agreement exists on the formal framework, as in the Western democracies, the usefulness of these norms in shaping events is high. But the importance of a constitution diminishes as the degree of its public acceptance declines, as is clearly the case in Chile. The majority of the parties consider the Chilean institutional order to be illegitimate, and they are willing to accept it, even in the best of cases, only as a point of departure for discussing its reform. In that sense, the Constitution of 1980 provides a weak basis for governance. Moreover, it contains a contradiction that may prove to be the seed of its own destruction. Within its rigid dictatorial structure, the constitution incorporates two elements that permit genuine political and popular social expression: elections and the creation of considerable political space. The constitution requires the transition period to culminate with a plebiscite. From this starting point, and despite its antidemocratic legal construction, the document recognizes political parties, elections, and a parliament, which together provide sufficient space for establishing electoral majorities and minorities. In sum, the plebiscite scheduled for the end of the transition period presents risks for the regime and possibilities for the opposition that cannot be analyzed strictly according to the formal structure of what the constitution does or does not stipulate.

Other countries' transitions to democracy have shown that the expression of popular sovereignty through elections is often a political act sweeping enough to devastate an authoritarian system. In this sense, analyses of various transitions from authoritarianism to democracy reveal that the key step may be achieving a sufficiently free election, even if this election is carried out within a constitutional framework created by the authoritarian regime. Transitional constitutional laws in post-fascist Spain, Portugal, and Italy were not legitimate in the sense that their origins were not democratic. Nonetheless, these bodies of law served as the basis for transitions to democracy.[3] The success of these transitions demonstrates that dictatorships are too institutionally fragile to restrain the popular will when expressed in a free and honest election—or somewhat free and honest. Spain, Uruguay, and Brazil are the most recent examples that illustrate this possibility. In contrast, the case of the Philippines closes the circle in a sense by showing that even a fraudulent election, in the face of a people mobilized around the demand for free elections, can be a catastrophe for a dictatorial regime.

Curiously, for the first time in fifteen years, Pinochet and the democratic opposition have agreed on a common stage for their struggle. Pinochet is betting on the possibility of keeping his regime in power through a plebiscite that will necessarily be fraudulent. The opposition believes that despite the state's overwhelming power, it is possible for Chilean society to express itself electorally, to defeat the military regime, and fortified by that victory, to sweep away the regime and its constitution. A majority of the citizenry will not accept being condemned to a ceremonial constitution that allows it no genuine power, confining it instead to an institutional structure where power is held by the military, not by the people.

In September 1987, at least a year before the as-yet-unscheduled plebiscite, internationally respected opinion polls recorded the views of the Chilean people. The results reflect the complex reality described in this book: the opposition had three times more support than Pinochet, yet most Chileans believed that the dictator would remain in power beyond 1989. The striking disparity between what Chileans consider politically desirable and what they consider possible offers dramatic testimony to the effects of fifteen years of "political recess" in a country once justly proud of its democratic tradition.

NOTES

Chapter 1

1. *Bando número 5* of the Junta de Gobierno de Chile, 11 Sept. 1973.
2. Ibid.
3. *Decreto-Ley número 1*, 11 Sept. 1973, *Acta de Constitución de la Junta de Gobierno*, published in *Diario Oficial*, 18 Sept. 1973.
4. Ibid.
5. *Inter-American Commission for Human Rights*, Organization of American States (OAS), *Report on the Status of Human Rights in Chile: Findings of "on the spot" Observations in the Republic of Chile, July 22–August 2, 1974* (Washington, D.C.: OAS General Secretariat, 1974).
6. *Decreto-Ley número 5*, 12 Sept. 1973.
7. Tomás Moulián and Pilar Vergara, *Políticas de estabilización y comportamientos sociales: la experience chilena, 1973–1978*, Apuntes CIEPLAN no. 22 (Santiago: CIEPLAN, 1979), p. 24.
8. *Decreto-Ley número 1*, 11 Sept. 1973.
9. *Qué Pasa*, no. 127 (Sept. 1973).
10. *Decreto-Ley número 128*, 12 Nov. 1973.
11. This event is also described in Augusto Pinochet's book *El día decisivo: 11 de septiembre 1973* (Santiago: Editorial Andrés Bello, 1979), 153. Pinochet, however, attributes Frei's not speaking to him to two different causes in different accounts: first, to Frei's annoyance at the Congress being shut down, and elsewhere, to Frei's unhappiness at having had his official car taken away from him (an explanation that reveals the mentality of Pinochet).

Chapter 2

1. Junta de Gobierno, *Declaración de principios del gobierno de Chile*, 11 Mar. 1974.
2. Ibid.
3. OAS, *Report on the Situation of Human Rights in Chile* (Washington, D.C.: OAS General Secretariat, 1985).
4. Ibid., 146.
5. *Decreto-Ley número 527*, 17 June 1974, Artículo 7.

6. Ibid., Artículo 18.
7. Ibid., Artículos 8 and 10.
8. *Decreto-Ley número 807*, 16 Dec. 1974, the single artículo.
9. *Decreto-Ley número 521*, 14 June 1974.
10. Florencia Varas, *Gustavo Leigh: el general disidente* (Santiago: Editorial Aconcagua, 1979), p. 78.
11. "Milton Friedman en Chile: bases para un desarrollo económico," text of the public lecture given in Santiago on 26 Mar. 1975 (Santiago: Fundación de Estudios Econónomicos BHC, Editorial Universitaria, 1975), p. 23.

Chapter 3

1. Junta de Gobierno, *Objectivo nacional del Gobierno de Chile*, disseminated by means of *Resolución 3.102*, 23 Dec. 1975, which states: "Approved as obligatory is the document named *Objetivo nacional de Chile....* The Ministers of State will be responsible for fulfilling the directives expressed in said document."
2. General Augusto Pinochet, *Mensaje presidencial*, 11 Sept. 1976.
3. Ibid.
4. Malú Sierra, "José Toribio Merino: Merino antes que gobernante," *Ercilla*, no. 2,165 (26 Jan.–1 Feb. 1977), pp. 20–24.
5. See Genaro Arriagada, *Ideology and Politics in the South American Military (Argentina, Brazil, Chile, and Uruguay*, Wilson Center Paper no. 55. See also Genaro Arriagada, *El pensamiento político de los militares*, 2d ed. (Santiago: Editorial Aconcagua, 1986).
6. See both works cited in the preceding note. On the sentence at the military trial, see Genaro Arriagada and Manuel Antonio Garretón, "América Latina a la hora de las doctrinas de seguridad nacional," private edition (Santiago: Centro de Investigaciones Socioeconómicas [CISEC] de la Compañía de Jesús en Chile, 1978), 197.
7. Augusto Pinochet, *Discurso en el Primer Aniversario del Gobierno*, 11 Sept. 1974.
8. Colonel Gerardo Cortés Rencoret, "Introducción a la Seguridad Nacional," *Cuadernos del Instituto de Ciencias Políticas* 2 (Feb. 1976): 23. The *Cuadernos* are published by the Universidad Católica in Santiago.
9. Augusto Pinochet, *Discurso en el Tercer Aniversario del Gobierno*, 11 Sept. 1976.
10. Roger Trinquier, *La guerra moderna* (Buenos Aires: Editorial Rioplatense, n.d.), 36–37.
11. Arriagada, *Ideology and Politics in the South American Military*, p.25.
12. OAS, *Report on the Situation of Human Rights in Chile* (1985).
13. Ibid., p. 111.

Chapter 4

1. Presentation by José Piñera E. in the seminar entitled "El empresario frente a la reactivación nacional," organized by the Department of Economics at the Universidad Católica de Chile, 19 May 1977.
2. Fernando Dahse, *El mapa de la extreme riqueza* (Santiago: Editorial Aconcagua, 1978).
3. Roberrto Zahler, "Repercussions monetarias y reales de la apertura al exterior: el caso chileno, 1975–1978," *Revista de la CEPAL* 10 (Apr. 1980).
4. See, for example, Claudio Orrego and Florencia Varas, *El caso Letelier* (Santiago: Editorial Aconcagua, 1979).
5. Heraldo Muñoz, *Las relaciones exteriores del Gobierno Militar Chileno* (Santiago: Ediciones del Ornitorrinco, 1986), 27.
6. Piñera presentation cited in note 1 above.
7. General Augusto Pinochet, speech delivered 9 July 1977 in the meeting organized at Chacarillas Hill by the Secretaría Nacional de la Juventud. The full text was presented in *El Mercurio*, 7 Feb. 1987.
8. See also the letter from Armando Fernández Larios to the vice-commander in chief of the Army, Santiago Sinclair, dated 21 Jan. 1987, in which he explains the reasons that led him to voluntarily turn himself in to U.S. authorities to clear up the question of his responsibility in the Letelier-Moffit killings. This letter was printed in full in *El Mercurio*, 7 Feb. 1987.
9. The complete text of this agreement is printed in Orrego and Varas, *El caso Letelier*, 123–25.
10. Interview in *Cosas*, 28 Sept. 1978, cited by Heraldo Muñoz in *Las relaciones exteriores*.
11. *Decreto-Ley número 527*, 11 Sept. 1979.
12. *Mensaje presidencial*, 11 Sept. 1979.
13. Ibid.

Chapter 5

1. Presentation on the state of Public Finance (Hacienda Pública), May 1980.
2. See *Hoy*, 24 Sept. 1980. Regarding this triumphal statement, see Pilar Vergara's excellent "Auge y caída del Neoliberalismo: un estudio sobre la evolución ideológica del régimen militar," FLASCO Documento de Trabajo no. 216, 1984. This citation and those following have been excerpted from Vergara's paper.
3. *El Mercurio*, 28 Aug. 1980.

4. Roberto Zahler, "Recent Southern Cone Liberalization Reforms and Stabilization Policies: The Chilean Case, 1974–1982," *Journal of Interamerican Studies and World Affairs* 25, no. 4 (Nov. 1983): 509–62.
5. Ricardo Ffrench-Davis, "El experimento monetarista en Chile: una síntesis crítica," *Estudios CIEPLAN* 9 (Dec. 1982):27.
6. Response of Alvaro Bardón, president of the Banco Central, quoted by Pilar Vergara, "Auge y caída del neoliberalismo," p. 253.
7. "La semana política," *El Mercurio*, 21 Sept. 1980.
8. *Decreto* 1065, 12 Nov. 1973.
9. Cited by Pilar Vergara, "Auge y caída del neoliberalismo," p.256.
10. *La Segunda*, 9 Sept. 1980, p. 1.
11. Interview in *Hoy*, 8 Sept. 1981.
12. For an analysis of the Constitution of 1980, see Genaro Arriagada Herrera, *Chile: el sistema político futuro* (Santiago: Editorial Aconcagua, 1980), 29ff.
13. Alejandro Silva Bascuñán, "Principios que informan la constitución política de 1980," *Revista Chilena de Derecho* 10, no. 2 (May–Aug. 1983):435.
14. *Constitution of 1980*, transitional article 15.

Chapter 6

1. José Pablo Arellano and René Cortázar, *Del milagro a la crisis: algunas reflexiones sobre el momento económico*, CIEPLAN Estudios no. 8 (Santiago: CIEPLAN, 1982).
2. Zahler, *Políticas recientes*, p. 321.
3. Aníbal Pinto, "La deuda externa y las (ir)responsabilidades compartidas," paper presented at the Conferencia sobre Deuda Externa, San José, Costa Rica, 9–11 Dec. 1985.
4. Arnold C. Harberguer, "La crisis cambiaria chilena de 1982," *Cuadernos de Economía* 21, no.63 (Aug. 1984):134, published by the Universidad Católica de Chile.
5. International Bank for Reconstruction and Development, "Chile, Economic Memorandum," 28 Sept. 1981, cited by Aníbal Pinto, "La deuda externa."
6. *El Mercurio*, 8 Nov. 1981.
7. E. Miller, "Micro-Economic Effects of Monetary Policy," quoted by Alejandro Foxley in *Hoy*, 21 Apr. 1982.
8. Patricio Silva Enchenique, "Enduedamiento interno y crisis financiera en Chile," CEPAL mimeo, 1985, pp. 5–6. This work offers an excellent analysis of the Chilean financial system in 1981–1983.
9. Alejandro Foxley y Dagmar Raczynski, *Grupos vulnerables en Situaciones recesivas: el caso de los niños y jóvenes chilenos*, Colección Estudios CIEPLAN, no. 13, p. 109.

10. René Cortázar, *Chile: resultados distributivos, 1973–1982*, Notas Técnicas CIEPLAN, no. 57, 1983, p. 12.

Chapter 7

1. Interesting work on the protests is beginning to appear. For example, see Gonzalo de la Maza and Mario Garcés, *La explosión de las mayorías: protesta nacional, 1983–1984* (Santiago: Educación y Comuncación [ECO], 1985); Alfredo Rodríguez, *Por una ciudad democrática* (Santiago: Ediciones Sur, 1984); Eduardo Valenzuela, *La rebelión de los jóvenes* (Santiago: Ediciones Sur, 1984); Genaro Arriagada Herrera, *Negociación política y movilización social: la crítica de las protestas* (Santiago: Centro de Estudios del Desarrollo [CED], Materiales para Discusión, 1987); Ignacio Balbontín, *Movilización social, control social de los conflictos y negociación política* (Santiago: CED, Materiales para Discusión, 1987); Hernán Pozo, *Partidos políticos y organizaciones poblacionales: una relación problemática*, FLACSO working paper (Santiago: FLACSO, 1986); and Philip Oxhorn, *Democracia y participación popular: organizaciones poblacionales en la futura democracia chilena*, FLACSO working paper (Santiago: FLACSO, 1986).
2. Manuel Antonio Garretón "Las complejidades de la transición invisible: movilizaciones populares y régimen militar en Chile," forthcoming in *Protest and Resistance Movements in Latin America*, edited by Susan Eckstein.
3. Eugenio Tironi, "Pobladores e integración social: resultados de investigación," manuscript.
4. Robert E. Dowse and John A. Hughes, *Political Sociology* (London: John Wiley and Sons, 1972), 422–23.
5. The most explicit justification of "what even the regime's spokespersons and press call pillage, ransacking, and vandalism" is found in the "Carta del Comité Central del Partido Comunista a los presidentes o secretarios generales de los partidos de oposición al régimen militar," mimeo, Sept. 1984. Also important is the February 1985 *Informe al Pleno del Comité Central del Partido Comunista*. The entire document is reprinted in Genaro Arriagada, Jaime Castillo, Eduardo Frei, and Radomiro Tomic, *La Democracia Cristiana y el Partido Comunista* (Santiago: Editorial Aconcagua, 1986), 233–308.
6. Javier Martínez, "Miedo al Estado, miedo a la socidad," *Proposiciones* 12 (Oct.–Dec. 1986).
7. Survey by Radio Cooperativa, the most important opposition medium of communications. This survey revealed that 63 percent of the low social stratum had supported the government's decision to declare a state of siege in November 1984, compared with 18 percent of the highest stratum.

8. Vicaría de la Solidaridad, *Noveno año de labor: 1984*, 47.
9. Ibid.

Chapter 8

1. The complete text of the founding document of the Democratic Alliance appears in the appendix of Gabriel Valdés, *Por la libertad* (Santiago: Centro de Estudios Sociales [CESOC], 1986), 323ff.
2. "Versión escrita del seminario [llamado] Un sistema jurídico-político constitucional para Chile," 27–28 July 1984, presentation of Senator Bulnes, mimeo issued by the Instituto Chilena de Estudios Humanísticos.
3. The Pinochet citations come from two articles by Blanca Arthur that appeared in *El Mercurio*: "La transición de Pinochet," 20 Jan. 1985, and "Pinochet y el año político," 5 Jan. 1986.
4. *Primer manifesto rodriguista al pueblo de Chile*, (N.p: n.p, 1985).
5. See *Informe al Pleno del Comité Central*, in Arriagada et al., *La Democracia Cristiana y el Partido Comunista*, 233–308.
6. Arthur, cited articles in *El Mercurio*, 20 Jan. 1985 and 5 Jan. 1986.
7. Ibid.
8. On these assassinations and the subsequent legal proceedings, see María Olivia Monckeberg, María Eugenia Camus, and Pamela Jiles, *Crimen bajo estado de sitio* (Santiago: Editorial Emisión, 1986).
9. Arthur, articles in *El Mercurio*, 20 Jan. 1985 and 5 Jan. 1986.
10. Letter from the National Directorate of the Christian Democratic party dated October 1984; and letter from Gabriel Valdés, president of the Christian Democratic party, to the Central Committee, 10 April 1985. The text of the second letter is reproduced in Arriagada et al., *La Democracia Cristiana y el Partido Comunista*, 203ff.
11. Letter from Gabriel Valdés, president of the Christian Democratic party, to Germán Correa and the Directorate of the Popular Democratic Movement, dated Jan. 1986. For the complete text, see Arriagada et al., *La Democracia Cristiana y el Partido Comunista*, 215ff.
12. The text can be found in Gabriel Valdés, *Por la libertad*, 323ff.
13. The complete text of the *Acuerdo nacional para la transición a la plena democracia* also appears in Valdés, *Por la libertad*, 337ff.
14. See Arthur articles in *El Mercurio*, 20 Jan. 1985 and 5 Jan. 1986.
15. On this crime, see Patricia Verdugo, *Quemados vivos* (Santiago: Editorial Aconcagua, 1986).
16. *El Mercurio*, 18 Sept. 1986.
17. On these assassinations, see Patricia Collyer and María José Luque, *José Carrasco, asesinato de un periodista* (Santiago: Editorial Emisión, 1987).

18. Letter from Gabriel Valdés, dated 10 Apr. 1985, reproduced in Arriagada et al., *La Democracia Cristiana y el Partido Comunista*, 203ff.

Chapter 9

1. General Carlos Prats, *Memorias: testimonio de un soldado* (Santiago: Pehuén Editores, 1985), 121ff.
2. Florencia Varas, *Conversaciones con Viaux* (Santiago: Talleres Impresiones Eire, 1972).
3. Prats, *Memorias*, 119.
4. *El Mercurio*, 10 May 1970.
5. *El Mercurio*, 8 May 1970.
6. *El Mercurio*, 10 May 1970.
7. See "Covert Action in Chile, 1963–1973: Staff Report of the Select Committee to Study Governmental Operations with Respect to Intelligence Activities," U.S. Senate, 94th Congress, 1st Session; also "Alleged Assassination Plots involving Foreign Leaders," U.S. Senate, 94th Congress, on the assassination of General René Schneider, pp. 225ff.
8. U.S. Senate report, *Alleged Assassination Plots Involving Foreign Leaders*, p.244.
9. Ibid., p. 225.
10. Arriagada, *El pensamiento político de los militares*, especially the chapter entitled "El ejército de Chile, la prusianización y la primera oleada antisocialista (1900–1931).
11. On the insurrectional faction within Popular Unity, see Genaro Arriagada Herrera, *De la vía chilena a la vía insurreccional* (Santiago: Editorial del Pacífico, 1974), 275ff. See also Claudio Orrego and Genaro Arriagada, *Leninismo y democracia* (Santiago: Editorial Aconcagua, 1976) and the works cited therein.
12. Prats, *Memorias*, 397.
13. Ibid., 402–3.
14. Ibid.
15. Ibid., 425.
16. Ibid., 423.
17. Ibid., 436.
18. General Augusto Pinochet Ugarte, *El día decisivo*, 119.
19. "Cómo llegaron las Fuerzas Armadas a la acción de 11 de septiembre de 1973?," *El Mercurio*, 11 Sept. 1974, special section, p. 10.
20. Ibid.
21. Sergio Arellano Iturriaga, *Más allá del abismo* (Santiago: Editorial Proyección, 1985), 43.
22. *El Mercurio*, "Cómo llegaron Las Fuerzas Armadas?", p. 15.

23. Ibid., p. 12.
24. Ibid., p. 16.
25. *Ercilla*, 26 Dec. 1973.
26. Pinochet, *El día decisivo*, 47.
27. Ibid., 78.
28. Ibid., 113.
29. Martin Needler, "Political Development and Military Intervention in Latin America," *American Political Science Review* 60 (Sept. 1966): 616–26.
30. Florencia Varas, *Gustavo Leigh*, 127–28.
31. Pinochet, *El día decisivo*, 78.
32. Ibid., 87.
33. Ibid., 101.
34. Ibid., 115.
35. Prats, *Memorias*, 495–96.
36. Joan Garcés, *El estado y los problemas tácticos en el gobierno de Allende* (Buenos Aires: Siglo Veintiuno Editores), 50.
37. Arellano Itarriaga, p. 45.
38. Ibid., 47–48.
39. Varas, *Gustavo Leigh*, 129–30.
40. President Raúl Alfonsín, speech given at the Cena Anual de Camaradería de las Fuerzas Armadas, published in the Buenos Aires daily *Clarín*, 6 July 1985.

Chapter 10

1. *Ercilla*, 11 Oct. 1973.
2. *Ercilla*, 21 Nov. 1973.
3. Interview by María Teresa Larraín published in the Argentine magazine *Panorama*, Dec. 1973.
4. *Ercilla*, 19 Dec. 1973.
5. *Ercilla*, 24 Apr. 1974.
6. *Qué Pasa*, 24 Oct. 1974.
7. *Ercilla*, 16 Jan. 1974.
8. *Ercilla*, Sept. 1973.
9. *Qué Pasa*, 25 Oct. 1973.
10. Juan Rial, *Partidos políticos, democracia y autoritarismo* (Montevideo: Centro de Informaciones y Estudios del Uruguay, Ediciones de la Banda Oriental, 1984), 2:55.
11. Karl von Clausewitz, *On War*, translated by Michael Howard and Peter Paret (Princeton, N.J.: Princeton University Press, 1976), 87 and 607.
12. Samuel Huntington, *The Soldier and the State* (New York: Vintage Books, 1957), 35.
13. Lieutenant General Benjamin Rattenbach, "Las Fuerzas Armadas y la política," *Documentos Internacionales* 67 (Nov. 1967–Feb. 1968):12.

14. General Ernesto Medina Fraguela, *Nuestra defensa nacional frente a la opinión pública* (Santiago: Benaprés y Fernández, 1941), 37–38.
15. Vice Admiral José Toribio Merino Suavedra, *La Armada Nacional y la dictadura militar: memorias del último Director General de la Armada* (Santiago: Imprenta Dirección General de Prisiones, 1932), 4.
16. Ibid., 48.
17. Zbigniew Brzezinski and Samuel Huntington, *Political Power: USA/USSR* (New York: Penguin Books, 1977), 332-333.
18. Huntington, *The Soldier and the State*, 101.
19. Andreas Dorpalen, "Hitler, el Partido Nazi y la Wehrmact en la Segunda Guerra Mundial," in *Poder civil y poder militar*, edited by Harry L. Coles (Buenos Aires: Editorial Hobbs-Sudamericana, 1970), 83.
20. Interview in *El Mercurio*, 16 Sept. 1979.
21. Interview by María Angélica Bulnes, *Qué Pasa*, 8 May 1980.
22. *Las Ultimas Noticias*, 26 Aug. 1983.
23. Interview by Elizabeth Subercauseux, *Cosas*, May 1981.
24. *El Mercurio*, 15 Oct. 1981.
25. Address given 23 Aug. 1983 to celebrate the tenth anniversary of Pinochet's appointment as commander in chief of the Army. The full text was published in *El Mercurio*, 24 Aug. 1983.
26. *El Mercurio*, 19 Sept. 1983.
27. Interview by Malú Sierra, *Cosas*, Sept. 1978.
28. Interview by Raquel Correa, *El Mercurio*, July 1981, emphasis in original.
29. Interview by Raqul Correa, *La Tercera*, Sept. 1980.
30. Interview by Raquel Correa, *El Mercurio*, July 1981.
31. Interview by Mónica Comandari, *Cosas*, Sept. 1984.
32. Ibid.
33. *El Mercurio*, 23 May 1982.
34. Speech of 23 Aug. 1986, published in *El Mercurio*, 24 Aug. 1986.
35. Ibid.
36. Ibid.
37. *El Mercurio*, 9 Sept. 1986.

Chapter 11

1. Philip M. Flammer, "Conflicting Loyalties and the American Military Ethic," in *War, Morality, and the Military Profession*, edited by Malham M. Wakin (Boulder, Colo.: Westview, 1979), 164–65.
2. Huntington, *The Soldier and the State*, 102–3.
3. Alain Roquié, *Poder militar y sociedad política en Argentina, 1943–1973* (Buenos Aires: Emecé Editores, 1982), 269.
4. Quoted by Roquié, *Poder militar*, 271.
5. Ibid., 270.
6. Virgilio Rafael Beltrán, "The Junta Level in Military Government: The Argentine Case," paper presented at the ninth World Congress

of Sociology, session of the Research Committee on Armed Forces and Society, Uppsala, Sweden, 14–19 Aug. 1978, p. 3.
7. Interview with General Roberto Viola by Malú Sierra, *Cosas*, June 1982.
8. Ibid.
9. Juan Rial, *Partidos políticos, democracia y autoritarismo* 2:55. In the same sense, see 1:83.
10. República Oriental del Uruguay, *Acta Institucional* 2, 12 June 1976.
11. República Federativa del Brasil, *Constitución política: texto completo y actualizado a 1976*, articles 90–93.
12. *O Estado de São Paulo*, 13 Oct. 1977.
13. *Decreto-Ley 1886*, 19 Aug. 1977.
14. Interview with General Washington Carrasco, *Qué Pasa*, 18 May 1980.

Chapter 12

1. *Decreto con Fuerza de Ley número 1* (1968), Article 166, Letter *e*.
2. *Decreto-Ley número 1639* (1976), published in *Diario Oficial*, 30 Dec. 1976.
3. *El Mercurio*, 20 Sept. 1978.
4. Interview in *El Mercurio*, 15 Oct. 1981.
5. *Decreto-Ley número 1640* (1976), published in *Diario Oficial*, 30 Dec. 1976.
6. Republic of Chile, *Constitución política del Estado*, Article 93 (Santiago: Editorial Jurídica de Chile, 1984).
7. Ibid.
8. Ibid., Article 96.

Chapter 13

1. General Medina Fraguela, *Nuestra defensa nacional*, 37–38.
2. *Decreto con Fuerza de Ley número 1* (1968), Chap. 5, Articles 74–98.
3. Ibid., Article 41.
4. *Decreto-Ley número 33*, 21 Sept. 1973, published in *Diario Oficial*, 23 Mar. 1974.
5. *Decreto-Ley número 220*, Article 2, 24 Dec. 1973, published in *Diario Oficial*, 23 Mar. 1974.
6. Ibid., Article 1, letter b.
7. *Decreto-Ley número 1052*, 2 June 1975, published in *Diario Oficial*, 7 June 1975.
8. *Decreto número 14 de la Subsecretaría de Guerra*, 4 Jan. 1977, delineated the revised, coordinated, and systematized text of the *Statute of Armed Forces Personnel*. The Extraordinary Selection Board was incorporated

as Paragraph 5 of Chapter 5 on assessments.

9. *Decreto con Fuerza de Ley número 1* (1968), Article 14.
10. *Decreto-Ley número 310*, 4 Feb. 1974, published in *Diario Oficial*, 9 Feb. 1974.
11. *Decree-Law número 1240*, Article 3, 28 Oct. 1975, published in *Diario Oficial*, 5 Nov. 1975.
12. Ibid., Article 1.
13. Ibid., Article 2.
14. *Decreto con Fuerza de Ley número 1* (1968), Article 1.
15. *Decreto-Ley número 624*, 26 Aug. 1974.
16. Ibid., Article 2, which replaces Article 79 of *Decreto con Fuerza de Ley número 1* (1968), final clause.
17. *Decreto-Ley número 1165*, 2 Sept. 1975.
18. Ibid., sole article, letter *a*, penultimate clause.
19. *Decreto-Ley número 624*, 26 Aug. 1974, Article 9, which combines Article 166bis with *Decreto con Fuerza de Ley número 1* (1968).
20. Medina Fraguela, *Nuestra defensa nacional*, p. 37.

Chapter 14

1. *Decreto-Ley número 1639* (1976).
2. *Decreto-Ley número 2956* (1979), published in *Diario Oficial*, 3 Dec. 1979, p. 1.
3. *El Mercurio*, 20 Sept. 1978.
4. *El Mercurio*, 6 June 1981.
5. *La Nación*, 6 Oct. 1984.
6. Ibid.
7. Ibid.
8. *Law Number 18,559*, 22 Sept. 1986.
9. Prats, *Memorias*, 568ff.
10. Ibid., 569.

Epilogue

1. Carlos Huneeus and Jorge Olave, "Autoritarismo y transición a la democracia: Chile en una perspectiva comparada," Centro de Estudios de la Realidad Contemporánea, Academia de Humanismo Cristiano, mimeo, 1986.
2. For an analysis of the Constitution of 1980, see Arriagada Herrera, *Chile: el sistema político futuro*.
3. Miguel Satrústegui, *El derecho constitucional transitorio*, FLACSO working paper (Santiago: FLACSO, 1984).

INDEX

189

Index

Calderón, General Alfredo 158, 160, 166
Canessa, Lieutenant General Julio 47, 113–15, 117, 133, 154, 158, 163, 165
Cánovas, Judge José 73
Carrasco, General Washington 98, 104, 113, 130, 133, 151–2, 154
Carter administration, relations with Pinochet regime 32, 35–6, 45
Carter, Hodding 35
Carvajal, Admiral Patricio 100–1
Carvajal, General Alfredo 86
Cassidy, Dr Sheila 14
Castellón, General Eduardo 159–60, 166
Castillo, General Sergio 151
Castillo, Jaime 46, 68
Castro, Sergio de 20, 28, 40, 52
Catholic Church, see Chile
Cauas, Jorge 20, 28, 52
Cauce 64–5
censorship 64
Central Bank 20, 28, 41, 51–4
Centro Nacional de Informaciones (CNI) 33, 161–2
Chacarillas Address 33–4
Chacón, General Hernán 161
Cheyre, General Emilio 86
Chicago Boys 15, 19–20, 28, 30, 40, 50, 52–3
Chile
  agriculture 30, 49, 52
  Air Force 16, 18, 36, 95–6, 107, 114
  Armed Forces
    corps of generals 150–5, 157–61, 163–4, 167
    duties of generals 165, 167
    intelligence services 17–18
    renaming of ranks 153, 155–7
    see also Chile, military
  Army 81–6, 88, 106–7, 115
    anticommunist tradition 86–8
    political involvement of 87–92, 101–2, 112–115, 137
    Prussian influence 87
  attempted coups 85–6, 90, 97
  banks 19–20, 28, 41, 51–4
  Catholic Church 10–11, 25, 75, 173
  child prostitution 54
  civilian–military relations 82–3
  civil liberties 66
  constitution 43–4

  see also Constitutions
  currency devaluation 8
  democracy 3–4
  drug addiction 54
  economic growth rate 49
  "economic miracle" 27–40, 49–50
  economic policies 3, 6–7
  see also Pinochet regime
  economic "shock treatment" 19–21
  financial conglomerates 52–3
  financial crisis 51–4
  financial institutions 51–2
  foreign competition 30
  foreign debt 3–4, 14, 32, 40–1, 50
  human rights 3, 6, 10, 13, 32, 54
    violation of, see Pinochet regime
  imports 41–2
  import tariffs 30
  industry 30, 49, 52–3
  inflation 6–8, 19–21, 49
  intelligence services 17–18
  interest rates 30
  international loans to 35–6, 41–2, 50–1
  labor confederations 172
  military
    arbitration 82
    career security 138, 140–1, 145–6, 148, 165–6
    coup 11 September 1973 3, 94–8, 100–1, 163
    posts 166
    promotions 138–48, 157, 159, 163–4, 167
    retirement rules 131–4, 138–43, 146, 153, 162
  Military Junta
    attitude of 102–4
    executive power in 106–7
    see also Pinochet regime
  mining 30, 49, 52
  monetarism 3, 15, 19
  National Police 16–18, 70, 73, 106–7, 113, 174
  national security doctrine 22, 25–6
  Navy 16, 18, 20, 95, 106–7
  opposition
    future of 174, 176–7
    international support for 173
    present strategy 175
    radio stations 65
    successes of 172–3
    see also Pinochet regime

Index

Index

Index

Index